östberg™

Library of Design Management

ADVANCE PRAISE FOR

HOW FIRMS SUCCEED, A FIELD GUIDE TO DESIGN MANAGEMENT

"Too many design professionals think that design excellence and financial acumen are mutually exclusive. Thanks to the authors of *How Firms Succeed* for putting this myth to rest. This book addresses the issues that, if practiced, will allow for both. One can only imagine the impact of a firm that provides best-of-class design and has the financial stability to continuously influence design and its impact on our communities."

RAYMOND F. MESSER, P.E., FACEC
President and Chairman,
Walter P. Moore and Associates, Inc.

"*How Firms Succeed* by Jim Cramer and Scott Simpson is a vital reference source for all design professionals. The skill with which they address the diverse needs of developing a critically acclaimed practice that is also a thriving business enterprise is particularly impressive. I'll make it 'required reading' for everyone in our firm."

LEO A. DALY III, FAIA, RIBA
Chairman and President, Leo A Daly Architecture, Planning, Engineering and Interior Design

"All too often design professionals get wrapped up in the grandness of the design and forget what the purpose of the commission was in the first place. They need to manage their relationships and finances with true professionalism. In our case we are improving the lives of millions of people and we want our architects and designers to be a part of the team with the same collective vision. *How Firms Succeed* is a book that helps achieve holistic health. It's enjoyable too. I think that Jim Cramer and Scott Simpson's book will be invaluable to the design professions and will be a great success itself."

PETE MCCAWLEY, AIA
President, PLJ Associates

"I loved this book! In these highly competitive times achieving success is just as much about running a quality business as it is about producing great design. *How Firms Succeed* provides deceptively simple, yet ultimately critical guidelines that apply to anyone seeking inspiration and insight—from young entrepreneurs just setting up practice to the senior management of well established firms needing that spark to rekindle new directions."

ROGER GODWIN, AIA, ASID
Principal and Managing Director, Gensler

"*How Firms Succeed*'s message is a particularly powerful one in these competitive times. Jim Cramer and Scott Simpson use a motivational approach that generates valuable ideas for firms of all sizes. This is the best precis of leadership in design firm management that I have ever read."

GARY WHEELER, FASID, FIIDA, ASSOC. AIA
Principal and Managing Director,
Perkins & Will

HOW FIRMS SUCCEED

A FIELD GUIDE TO DESIGN MANAGEMENT

HOW FIRMS SUCCEED

A FIELD GUIDE TO DESIGN MANAGEMENT

JAMES P. CRAMER & SCOTT SIMPSON

FOREWORD BY HON. RICHARD SWETT, FAIA

GreenwayConsulting

östberg

Östberg Library of Design Management

LCCN: 2001098417
ISBN: 0-9675477-8-4

Greenway Communications
a division of The Greenway Group, Inc.
30 Technology Parkway South, Suite 200
Atlanta, GA 30092
(800) 726-8603
www.greenwayconsulting.com

This book is dedicated to Corinne Cramer and
Nancy Kuziemski, whose encouragement, support
(and tolerance!) made this book possible.
They are truly best-of-class.

CONTENTS

THE ANATOMY OF LEADERSHIP

ACKNOWLEDGEMENTS

T he success of any enterprise rests in the people who help make it happen, and this book is no exception. *How Firms Succeed: A Field Guide to Design Management* is a search for the best and most effective ideas that are accelerating the evolution of the design professions. In the course of this journey we have been blessed by the contributions, inspiration, and feedback of dozens of the best and brightest thinkers from around the world.

It is always risky business to begin thanking people, because inadvertently (but inevitably) someone gets overlooked. However, this is a risk worth taking.

We are grateful to architect and U.S. Ambassador Richard Swett, whose foreword so aptly crystallizes the purpose and mission of this book. Special mention also goes to the members of The Design Futures Council, whose business it is to see over the horizon and conceptualize what's coming next. Our thanks to Connie Eggleston, Phil Bernstein, Arol Wolford, Curtis Allen, and Doug Parker. Other DFC board members to whom we owe thanks include April Thornton, Gary Wheeler, Jim Follett, Paul Doherty, Roger Godwin, Steve Fiskum, Janet Martin, Gordy Mills, Neil Frankel, Friedl Bohm, Harold Adams, Bill Dye, and Meritt Seymour. We also thank Tom Galloway, Alex "Sandy" Pentland, Harrison Fraker, Cecil Steward, and Ray Yeh. Each have inspired us with their ideas, vision, and critical thinking.

The leaders and staff of the world's leading design associations have also been supportive. We thank the AIA, ASLA,

ACEC, IIDA, IDSA, SEGD, ASID, SDA, RIBA, JIA, DBIA, SMPS and many other organizations that have cooperated and shared with us their insights and knowledge. And we appreciate the many opportunities to speak at their national meetings and interact with their members; we've learned a great deal in the process.

Critical review of the text by some of our clients and colleagues was especially helpful. We wish to thank Pete McCawley, former director, Global Real Estate at Amgen, who helped invent, test, and prove that many of the techniques mentioned here actually work, and Kevin Sharer, CEO of Amgen, who provided a real-life project as a beta test (even though he didn't know it at the time!). Special thanks to Ray Messer, Rod Kruse, Dan Avchen, and Leo A. Daly III.

We are also grateful to our colleagues at *DesignIntelligence*, the breeding ground for many of the ideas and much of the early text. We are thankful to our colleagues at The Stubbins Associates, The Greenway Group, and Counsel House Research for their encouragement and indulgence as the book was taking shape.

To Scott Carde, our speaking partner at numerous seminars at which these ideas were first expressed; to Joe Pine, whose ideas about "the experience economy" are reshaping how design gets done; and to Jim Walsh of Walsh Bros. Construction, who actually builds the castles that architects dream about, we are eternally grateful.

Thanks also to Richard Fitzgerald, leader of the Boston Society of Architects, and Beverly Hauschild-Baron, executive of the Minnesota Society of Architects, who have provided many a podium with which to present our ideas and challenge our concepts.

We also wish to thank John Seely Brown, whose innovative thinking is helping to reshape the nature of work. Also, one of the co-founders of The Design Futures Council, the late Jonas Salk, whose capacity to inspire wonder and curiosity was boundless and inspired the tone and attitudes in the book. We are indebted to our friend Dr. Richard Farson, whose instinct for leadership, good humor (and good scotch) will never be forgotten.

To Peter Beck and the staff of The Beck Group, who shared their innovative business models and gave us an opportunity to examine issues of value migration and innovation in the evolution of professional services, we are most grateful.

We wish to thank the following firms for their assistance: IDEO, Hammel Green and Abrahamson, HLKB, Gensler, ASD, SOM, Perkins & Will, Durrant, Ewing Cole Cherry Brott, Polshek Partnership, Dujardin Design Associates, and The Stubbins Associates. And we are grateful to CAMA, Foster Partnership, Cesar Pelli Architects, Morris Architects, Michael Graves and Associates, Henning Larson of Copenhagen, Damianos Group, Richard Rogers, Fumihiko Maki, CommArts, RTKL, NBBJ, Jova Daniels Busby, Frankel + Coleman, Santiago Calatrava, Kahler Slater, and so many others for sharing stories.

To Jennifer Evans Yankopolus, whose cheerful and organized editing kept us on track; to Austin Cramer, whose delightful cartoons and infectious humor always hit the mark; to Jennie Monahan whose thorough and meticulous layout skills helped us give shape to the book and to Mary Pereboom, Beth Seitz, Kerry Harding, Lee Cuthbert, Lisa Ashmore, Chelsea Butler, and Bret Witter of Greenway Consulting, who all contributed content, ideas, and joy to the project in their own special ways. We are indebted to each of you more than you know.

We would also like to acknowledge Dr. John Silber of Boston University, the son of an architect, as one of this country's great clients, and Thom Penney of LS3P, the 2003 President of The American Institute of Architects. And to the hundreds of architects, engineers, and designers who embraced this project from the beginning and supported us along the way with stories of both successes and failures. You have been patient and generous with us and helped us learn. Thanks for sharing your visions and secrets. This has been inspirational as we have come to appreciate how each problem also contains the seed of a solution, which can lead to success, satisfaction, and most certainly, design excellence.

We take special pleasure in presenting a book which addresses the question of how firms and professionals can "redesign design" to create more value for their clients and more satisfaction for themselves in the process. We hope that this book will help you to achieve your dreams.

James P. Cramer, Atlanta, GA
Scott Simpson, Cambridge, MA

FOREWORD XIX

HON. RICHARD SWETT

I have long believed that the architecture profession needs exactly what this book provides—namely a top notch guide to the pragmatic dimensions of running a successful design firm. There are precious few books that address this topic at all. Most books on architecture deal with buildings as art objects and focus on the design aspects of the structure. *How Firms Succeed* by Jim Cramer and Scott Simpson is an invaluable resource book that transforms the poetry of architecture into the prose of practical management advice. This book will give any firm greater organizational and business confidence to optimize their design capabilities because it answers and offers solutions to many of the questions and problems that distract firms from their quest to provide excellent design.

During the course of my career as an architect, energy developer, congressman, and ambassador, I have witnessed and participated in a maze of complex systems, governmental regulations, professional disciplines, special interest groups, grassroot community organizations and big businesses, all seeking to impact our "built environment." I have found that there are few people well equipped to sort through the cacophony of competitive interests in a constructive way that ultimately achieves harmony. By virtue of our training, skills and perspective, designers should play that role, but sadly, they rarely do.

From this morass of conflict, architects and designers are expected to create sound structures of lasting value—works of ART, if you will. These forms we create are more than art, however. They must function as protective machines providing order and place while they elevate the human condition, both spiritually and literally. And, as we all know, this is easier, much easier, said than done. But that IS what we architects, engineers, and designers are committed to do—it is the central mission of our design professions.

Daunting as this mission is, the truth is that in today's world what I have just described is no longer enough. We must be prepared to do more. It is time that every architect with the vision and desire to create outstanding designs must also be able to successfully administer his or her practice so that the firm's creations are the best they can be. Today, architecture and engineering is much more than just the design of buildings. It is a process that has the responsibility to organize and interpret complex quantities of information that include not only the physical creation of the building, but an incorporation of all the systems, infrastructure, relationships between people and information that are contained within as well. In addition to this, the building must respond to and enhance the context of the community in which it is located.

This is a tall order for any architect and client to address successfully. That is why every firm engaged in this exciting and important task needs to first insure that the administrative responsibilities are taken care of. In *How Firms Succeed*, any architect, engineer, or designer who is managing a firm can find a truly comprehensive collection of accessible and useful descriptions of the multitude of components that go into making a firm successful. Many of the examples are taken from profitable practices that are leading the profession in innovative design and management techniques. The book is a tremendous user's guide that every firm should possess.

In its pages are not only descriptions of examples and techniques used in some of the nation's leading firms but helpful lists of important organizational tools that bring light and reason to the managerial requirements any firm must address. Whether it is understanding how to market a firm's abilities, operating the business, providing the professional services or adequately balancing the risks and rewards of the financial aspects of a practice, Jim Cramer and Scott Simpson use their wealth of experience and professional training to describe in manageable detail all this useful information in a way that is tailored to the architect's particular needs.

The closing chapter of the book, "Anatomy of Leadership," eloquently addresses an issue that I believe is of central importance to the architecture profession—leadership. Architects, engineers, and designers can and must be leaders in the public life of their communities, and Cramer and Simpson's book furthers the discussion how and why. This book should rapidly become an indispensable part of every designer's working library.

"The future is already here; it's just not evenly distributed."

WILLIAM GIBSON

Design can be a schizophrenic business. It's both an art and a science, depending equally on creativity and constraint. It's a blend of the real and the symbolic—both tangible and ethereal. It's the most public of the arts, but it is often practiced in solitude.

Designers seek the illusion of control, but their real power is merely the power of persuasion. Architects and engineers consistently rank among the most admired and trusted of all professionals, but at the same time, many complain that their clients don't understand them, their fees are too low, and their ideas are too often ignored or misinterpreted by the public.

There can be great joy in design, but the frustrations are equally acute. There is no perfect site, program, or budget, and since the clients who commission projects are real people, it is impossible to make them perfectly happy. There is a chronic tug-of-war between aspirations and available resources. One of the great ironies of design is that there are more solutions than there are problems, and so only a very small percentage of good ideas ever becomes real. All of these factors make for interesting psycho-dynamics in the design profession.

To a large degree, the psychology of design is rooted in the academy. Academicians, relatively few of whom are practicing professionals, tend to romanticize the design process, preferring to believe that genius thrives best in the ivory tower, unencumbered by practical considerations or constraints. They rightly resist the notion that they are engaged in running trade schools, whose primary goal is to prepare students to earn a living. (As a corollary, law schools teach about the law, and not necessarily how to be a good lawyer.) The message of academia is that one must choose between being a "pure" designer, totally and completely devoted to the art of design, or being successful in practice, which implies compromising one's ideals for the sake of making a profit. (It should be noted that total and complete devotion to design doesn't guarantee either talent or result, and that there are many examples of wonderful architects who are also perfectly capable of balancing a checkbook.)

In design school, there are simply too many things to teach, and too little time to adequately prepare students in all aspects of professional practice. Still, it is unfortunate that the imperatives of "real life" are too often ignored or glossed over in the classroom, as if such things as budgets and building codes are mere speed bumps in how "real design" gets done. As a result, emerging generations of designers too often carry the baggage of unrealistic expectations, leading to confusion and resentment, not only with themselves but also with their clients.

Is there an inevitable conflict between business skills and design talent? There need not be, and this book explains techniques and tips for a unifying logic that brings design and business skills into satisfying balance. Facts are facts—regardless of individual talent, there are some things that everyone needs to know about running a successful design practice, or else all that valuable training is at risk of going to waste.

The problem is not that good design and good business don't go together (they do!)—the problem lies with the prevailing paradigm of professional practice and how it is communicated not only to the next generation of professionals but to the public at large. The blend of art and business in design is much misunderstood. In fact, many of the "problems" faced by designers are not problems at all but merely misplaced perceptions.

The truth is that design encompasses much more than appearance, which is too often merely skin deep. Good design goes far beyond color, texture, material, and proportion. In architecture, it includes the strategy behind a building *(why is it being built?)*, the technology of a building *(what is it made of and how is it put together?)*, the economics of a building *(who will pay for it and how much will it cost to maintain over its useful life?)*, and the politics *(what approvals or variances are required and who will grant them?)*.

Finally, and perhaps most importantly, design is made by people—most often teams of people—whose work is a function of not only talent but also leadership, management, communication, and collaboration. The human dynamics involved in producing good design should not be underestimated.

All of these factors weigh heavily on both process and result. Seen this way, design is something like Rubik's Cube: the organizing principles and the mechanism are relatively simple but it is devilishly difficult to align all the colors simultaneously.

What the profession needs is a model that explains how the mechanics of the successful design firm actually work—a certain simplicity that shines through all the complexity. As Justice Byron White famously said of pornography, we may not be able to define great design, but we know it when we see it (and we also know when it's missing). People in all walks of life understand that good design is not only beautiful, but it enhances productivity, makes the best use of valuable resources, is cost effective, contributes to our sense of community, carries symbolic and emotional weight, and raises our spirit. In a sense, everyone is an architect, because we all have a role and a stake in shaping our environment and the quality of daily life.

Good design reflects what we are as a culture and what we care about as a society. Our greatest buildings have become our icons—the fruits by which we are known. These are the compelling reasons why people care so much about design, and it's one of the reasons architects are traditionally admired and respected by the public at large. Why is it, then, that practitioners have such a hard time explaining the value of what they do and such a hard time doing it?

Shaping the Future of Design Management

Since there is so much demonstrable value in good design, it would seem that the organizational aspects of professional practice would be second nature.

But that is not the case. The frustrations felt by practitioners are real, and they are exacerbated by the tremendous changes that are surging through the professions. One of the most obvious is the impact of technology. To understand the enormity of this shift, it should be remembered that CAD drafting, e-mail, voice mail, project Web sites, teleconferencing, and cell phones simply did not exist when the principals of most of today's major firms were in training. Technology has crushed conventional standards, and created a whole new set of expectations about what is possible and how long things

should take. As a result, there are three important shifts that
have irrevocably altered the design and construction industry.

1. **The first major shift is *connectivity*.** Because of technology, more people are more accessible more of the time. Out-of-town no longer means out of touch. As a consequence, there is an unspoken and pervasive assumption that team members are always fully and completely informed, despite the fact that e-mail, voice mail and faxes are not always instantly received and processed. We falsely assume that if it's been sent, it's been read, understood, and acted upon. Ubiquitous access means that clients, architects, consultants, and contractors are constantly swimming in a sea of information with the inevitable consequence that managing information flow has become a new and necessary design skill. Designers do not habitually see themselves as information managers, but technology demands that this be added to their repertoire. Those who ignore or downplay this imperative do so at their peril. Technology is changing fast, and design professionals are expected to be up to speed, regardless of what zip code or time zone they inhabit.

2. **The second major shift is *speed*.** Because things *can* be done faster, it is expected that they *will* be done faster. The opportunity to take extra time to contemplate subtleties is increasingly rare, which is understandable when one considers how fast clients must run their businesses to simply stay in place. Like connectivity, speed in and of itself is not necessarily a bad thing, but it must be understood to be properly managed. While it is not always true that the first idea is the best idea, neither is it true that taking more time

guarantees higher quality (many a cake has been ruined by being left in the oven too long). The ability to produce things better, faster, and cheaper is a strategic skill and quite counterintuitive to the culture of design that is nurtured in the academy.

Now more than ever, designers need to get comfortable with the tools and technologies that make increased speed both possible and desirable. These new tools and technologies are like the *Mayflower* or the *Apollo* spacecraft—they take us to new worlds and make us see our once-familiar surroundings with entirely different eyes. Speed changes the very nature of what's possible.

3. **This leads us to the third major shift:** *productivity*. How does productivity relate to design quality? Productivity is important because it invites us to consider the difference between process and result. The "traditional" design process was based on tracing paper, parallel rules, and cardboard models, and it took a certain amount of time. The new design process is based on bits and bytes, and all it takes is nanoseconds.

New design technologies have given birth to different ways of conceptualizing space, and so it should come as no surprise that architects, engineers, and designers are beginning to explore forms that until recently could only exist in the imagination—sinuous curves, sharp angles, syncopated juxtapositions—extremely complex forms that seem to have been imported from another solar system. Without enhanced technology and productivity, none of this would be possible.

"Our growth increase in corporate performance seems to coincide with the decision to hire these architects."

In this brave new world, where connectivity, speed, and productivity have changed all the old rules, a new kind of design firm is being born. This new firm understands that design, at its root, is about creating value. This new firm sees architecture as a social art, made by and for people. This new firm is respectful of the past, yet eager to explore new territory. This new firm understands the relationship between process and result, and especially appreciates the fact that as a profession, *design itself is being redesigned.*

Under a new paradigm, the Design/Enterprise model, there is no upside limit to success—it only depends upon how far designers want to push the envelope.

Envisioning the Future

What does this new firm look like? How is it organized? What makes it work? The fundamental organizing principles are relatively simple and easily understood, but the variety of

8

HOW FIRMS SUCCEED

THE DESIGN/ENTERPRISE MODEL

possible solutions is vast. Regardless of the size, location, or special focus of a design firm, there are only four basic things that are necessary for success. If any one of the four is missing, the firm's performance will be marginalized. To the extent the four factors are in balance, there is no constraint to growth or success. Tomorrow's professional leaders understand these essentials and are acting on them.

    1. **The first key success factor is *marketing*.** Simply defined, marketing is the process by which firms identify, create, and retain clients and projects. It should be obvious that without clients, there is nothing for a firm to do, and yet

this most basic of skills is often ignored in graduate school. Whether a firm is large or small, regional or national, generalist or narrowly focused, *all* projects start with successful marketing. A firm without clients is like a hospital without patients.

"Marketing" is sometimes seen as a dirty word in the profession—it implies that slick salesmanship is a substitute for design quality. Nothing could be further from the truth. Instead, marketing must be seen for what it really is—the essential connection between a firm's skills and the needs of the marketplace. It's how firms declare to all comers that *"this is what we do, this is what we're good at, and this is how we can help you be successful."* Seen this way, marketing is the very first step in the design process. It is the process by which the designer comes to understand the goals and aspirations of the client. Without this essential connection *("we understand you...")* the probability of producing good design is greatly diminished. There are many marketing techniques that can be easily taught and easily learned. Effective marketers come in all shapes, sizes, and styles; no one need undergo a personality transplant to become a good marketer. All that is required is honesty, directness, and a sincere desire to harness the power of design to help the client. These are the essential ingredients of marketing credibility. Only when the commission is secured can the next step in the design process take place.

2. **This leads to the second success factor:** *operations.* Operations is the process by which the work gets organized. Space must be rented, furniture procured, computers networked, office policies devised, staff hired and trained,

leadership established. Without these essentials, even successful marketing will be of little value. Operations creates the context in which good design can thrive, and like marketing, it is very much a design activity. In marketing, we learn how to "design" client relationships. In operations, we "design" process. In a sense, operations is like painting the lines on a tennis court and stringing up the net—it establishes the parameters and boundaries by which the game is played. Without rules to guide the design effort, all that results is chaos. Operations are one of the most powerful design skills, but like marketing, it's routinely overlooked and under-appreciated.

3. **Once the commission has been secured and the workplace protocols established, the third success factor kicks in:** *professional services*. Simply put, this is doing the actual work, and the actual work is not just drawing lines on paper. The design process includes analyzing relevant data, researching codes and regulations, conceptualizing possible solutions, expressing design ideas in drawings and models (both tangible and electronic), coordinating the activities of various team members both inside and outside the office, coordinating and transmitting vast amounts of information, convincing the client to make key decisions, and finally bringing the process to closure—hopefully on time and within budget.

To accomplish all this, teams of highly skilled people are needed, and so professional services also concerns itself with communication, management, and leadership. At the end of this process, there must be a defined result, and what makes this especially tricky is that while there are many options from which to choose only one final solution will actually get built. The truly proficient designer understands this and is courageous enough to commit, heart and soul, to a given solution (and is able to convince others to commit as well). Without this buy-in, there is no closure and hence no actionable design.

It should be pointed out that in the world of architecture, the designer provides the instructions but does not actually build the building. Thus, drawings, models and specifications are not an end in themselves, they are merely instruments of service that enable other team members like construction managers and contractors to do their jobs well. This essential fact should shape how professional services are conceived and delivered, and it opens up possibilities for new and different kinds of services that were not previously considered to be in the designer's province.

Because of technology, professional services are delivered more and more by means of bits and bytes—they take up essentially no space, can be easily manipulated and edited, and cost almost nothing to reproduce. This only serves to underscore that *the essential value designers provide comes in the form of ideas that inspire action in others.*

4. **While the marketing, operations, and professional services are the first three critical steps in the success model, they mean nothing at all without the fourth success factor:** *finance.*

Once again, this has a simple but compelling definition—finance is about collecting and managing money. This involves timesheets, expenses, invoices, payments to consultants, managing operational expenses, etc. Money is the fuel that enables the design enterprise to operate; without it, no designer, no matter how brilliant or clever, can sustain a firm. Like design itself, money is many things—a means of exchange, a measure of value, and sometimes an end in itself. It is also a fundamental design tool. Money has an emotional content, and it means different things to different people. Some are able to talk about money only with a measure of discomfort—it's a subject to be avoided if at all possible—while others understand that money is just a commodity. Like speed, it means very little all by itself. What matters is how it is put to use.

"Money" is a foreign language to many design professionals. It's not part of the standard curriculum in design schools. And yet, money is the standard language of business and finance, and most clients speak this language quite fluently. To communicate effectively with clients, it behooves all designers who are interested in being as influential as possible to learn this foreign tongue and speak it fluently. Why? Because money is a force that in some way shapes the outcome of all projects. To get the very best out of a design opportunity, it's necessary to know what things cost; this is the only way to maximize the resources available. Thus, the use of money is strategic, and very much a legitimate tool of the designer, just like a pencil.

These four firm fundamentals—*marketing, operations, professional services,* and *finance*—are akin to the four basic chemical instructions encoded in DNA, the universal language of human biology. They are simple, they are essential, and they can be combined in a huge variety of ways to create infinite choices. They provide the means and the methods for designers to engage their talents in the most productive ways. A firm that truly understands and acts on these essentials will have a significant strategic advantage over more conventional firms—it will not only understand its own business but will also understand its clients' business. Making the connection between the two is key to success, and that's what this book is all about.

austin © 2003
for DesignIntelligence

MARKETING:
GETTING THE WORK

The first requirement in doing good design is getting the commission. "Marketing" is the process used to make the essential connection between the passion and talent of the design firm and the needs of the marketplace. Without this essential connection, your talent will go to waste. Thus, marketing is the first essential step in the design process. Through marketing, you become intimately familiar with your clients and come to understand their aspirations. It's how you learn about opportunities and constraints—the parameters of budget, schedule, and scope of work that govern each and every project, no matter how large or small. Successful marketing is based on a few sound principles—good listening, clear communication, credibility, and follow through. Contrary to popular opinion, marketing does not require a personality transplant. Anyone who is properly motivated can do it well—all you need to do is put the needs of your client first and foremost, and the rest will follow.

TARGET MARKETING: PURSUING THE RIGHT PROJECTS

"Marketing success depends on both what you do and how you do it…if you don't have a strategic advantage, create one."

PETER BECK

The purpose of marketing is to identify, attract and retain clients for the firm. This can take a variety of forms, including public relations, responding to RFPs, conducting interviews, making presentations, and social contact with clients. Smart marketing is a strategic investment, and your goal should be to produce maximum results for the investment required.

How much does marketing cost, and what is it actually worth? These are two questions that drive the value proposition when assessing the overall effectiveness of your marketing program. To get the answers, start with the fundamental principle that if it costs more to bring in a job than you can earn by doing it, then your marketing—no matter how successful—will eventually drive you out of business.

In any given year, there is far more business to be done than your firm can do alone, and you will never capture 100 percent of the market. Therefore, one of the first and most important things that you can do to improve your marketing effectiveness is to choose your targets carefully—pursue only those projects for which you are uniquely qualified or well connected. In other words, your best marketing strategy is to focus your energy on the work that you truly want. Resist the temptation to be greedy.

A few firms have long waiting lists of clients with significant projects, but most are not so fortunate. There is a story, perhaps apocryphal, about Philip Johnson. A famous client sent Johnson an RFP, and in return received the shortest winning proposal in history: "I'll do it." And he did. But most often, responding to RFPs is seldom simple. Wasting time chasing jobs that you aren't likely to get and don't want anyway diverts important time and attention from the core mission of the firm. Such diversion is extraordinarily expensive, so avoid it at all costs.

To get a handle on how to choose, do a little research to determine your true "cost of sales." The cost of sales measures the expenditure required to capture a dollar's worth of new fees, including both time and materials. This can be done firm wide for specific markets or for individual projects. Most firms devote approximately seven to eight percent—and sometimes as much as ten percent—of their annual net revenue to marketing, which means that their cost of sales ranges from seven to ten cents on the dollar. The true figure can be actually much higher when opportunity cost is factored in, meaning that activities devoted to pursuing a project unsuccessfully are doubly expensive because that effort could have been used to support ongoing profitable projects. Not only do you lose the prospective job; you forgo project revenue in the process.

When you have computed your true cost of sales, compare it to your profit margins. This will tell you instantly which of the various market segments, projects and clients make the most sense for your firm. Are your margins covered by your marketing? If not, something is amiss, so find out what and fix it.

The best and most productive marketing will occur when you are able to make a fit between the true talent of the firm and the true needs of the marketplace. Be honest about what you do well, celebrate it, and successful marketing will follow naturally.

QUESTIONS

1. What is your true cost of sales?

2. What is your firm's hit rate in attracting new clients?

3. Based on actual results, who are your most effective marketers?

4. Before chasing a project, how will you know that you should?

MARKETING: SETTING THE TEMPO

"No man is wise enough by himself."

PLAUTUS

Marketing works best if you invest your personal energy to make it a normal everyday part of your office culture. Reinforce the message that marketing is the first and most important step in the design process by starting each week with a Monday morning marketing meeting. Your message to your staff will be something like this: "Marketing is a team process. We should never stop looking, learning, and growing in ways that will strengthen our marketing and sales efforts. We'll meet weekly to review our marketing agenda and to challenge ourselves so that we don't get too comfortable, familiar, and stale."

At the meeting, we've found that it helps the focus of the discussion to issue a simple summary, updated each week, that lists the short-term and longer-term leads that you're chasing, a record of the wins and the losses, and a graph that shows your progress (both the hit-rate and the expenditures) benchmarked against your annual targets. This way, you'll know at a glance if you're "above-the-line" (ahead on wins and below budget), or "below-the-line" (watch out…you'll feel the effects three months down-the-line!). Most importantly, each participant should make a brief oral report about current leads and contacts, recent marketing intelligence, and the strategy for specific clients and projects; five minutes each should do.

You'll be surprised at how much this information sharing does to increase overall marketing effectiveness, because it makes marketing a team effort and gives everyone a chance to contribute to overall success. Make sure that your marketing meetings are held in a visible place—the staff should know what's going on and why—and encourage anyone in the firm who can make a contribution to attend.

The important thing is to demystify marketing. Make it everyone's business to help get work for the firm. Show by example that you value marketing and that you'll provide additional training for those who are especially interested or talented in this area. It's one of the best investments you can make.

QUESTIONS

1. How can you instill marketing as a firm-wide value?

2. Who should attend your weekly marketing meetings?

3. How do you quantify marketing success?

4. How will you get younger staff involved in marketing?

THE LANGUAGE OF MARKETING—A NEW GRAMMAR

"The limits of my language mean the limits of my world."

LUDWIG WITTGENSTEIN

A rchitects and designers are often criticized as having weak business and financial skills. Along with poor listening and arrogance, business and financial skills are cited by clients as one of the biggest shortcomings of design professionals. This is not a new area of criticism; it has lingered like a cloud for many years. What should be done?

One alternative, of course, is to ignore the issue altogether. Another is to turn it into an unexpected advantage. Why not candidly and radically (but politely) make "business grammar" part of your overall brand identity? Why not hit clients right between the eyes with pragmatic business concerns and issues? Why not invest the time and energy to wow your clients by talking business in ways that are especially relevant to them? Here are three techniques that will help you do just that.

1. **Talk business talk.** Read your local business journal and two to three business papers, such as *Investors Business Daily, Financial Times* and the business section of *The New York Times*. Scan *Fast Company, Business Week*, and *Fortune* and select one or two relevant articles to read each week.

Then, write down three key points and add those to your daily conversations with clients and colleagues. Make this a lasting habit.

2. **Never simply "comply" with a client request.** Create a dialogue of value. Always respond with options and ideas that demonstrate how much you can benefit the client's bottom line. Think about this as managing expectations toward a new level of respect for design and your business value to the client. Always deliver what you promise and then provide an unexpected enhancement. Your long-term and repeat business will soar.

3. **Be direct and avoid wasteful processes.** Your process skills as a designer are often misused. Clients frequently complain that architects and designers take inefficient or unrealistic approaches to problems and entertain false assumptions. On the other hand, those who stand out have done their homework and understand the client's values, resources, and constraints. They know the right questions to ask. And nothing pleases a client more than knowing that the architect knows and cares about the bottom line —not to the exclusion of design but as a value when current. Take this challenge and you will stand out from the crowd.

1. How will you make business grammar a part of your firm's brand identity?

2. How will you respond to clients with value-added proposals?

3. How will you better understand your client's needs in order to stand out from other firms in your market?

4. How can you use business terms more often in your design practice?

MARKETING: SETTING THE BUDGET

"In the long run, men hit only what they aim at. Therefore, they had better aim at something high."

HENRY DAVID THOREAU

One of the most important concepts about marketing is that it needs to be cost effective. You can't live without it, but if you spend too much money bringing a job into the office, then even if you're successful in doing the work, you'll eventually drive yourself out of business. In evaluating your marketing costs, focus on your "cost of sales." Simply put, this tells you how much you have to spend to bring in every dollar of new fees. Though this varies by firm size and type, most offices spend around seven to eight cents on the dollar to produce new work. (And remember that if your cost of sales for a project exceeds your profit margin for that work, you are on the road to failure.)

Here's a simple way to create a pro-forma marketing budget. If you are an architecture firm, multiply the total number of staff in your office by $125,000 (the standard per employee revenue benchmark for architecture firms) and set your marketing budget at seven percent of that figure. Remember that this must cover both labor and expenses. Then set your targets accordingly. For example, a 50-person firm will have to produce $6.25 million in new fees (50 times $125,000) and spend no more than $437,500 in marketing labor and material in order to have an effective marketing program. Keep within these parameters and you'll do fine.

While tracking your progress with regard to new booked work and ongoing costs, don't forget that it's OK to exceed the marketing budget as long as you have the results to show for it. For example, you may choose to spend an additional $50,000 to pursue a dream project—this is no problem *as long as you win*, but you must resist the temptation to spend marketing money based mainly on hope. To make the marketing budget work, you must exercise true discipline. This means that *not* going after a low-probability job is one of the best marketing decisions that you can make. Instead, save those precious dollars for targets you have a good chance of hitting. In other words, use a rifle, not a shotgun.

Here are some useful benchmarks when considering your marketing strategy:

1. The hit rate (ratio of new projects won as a percentage of those chased) should be at least 30 percent, meaning that you should get one out of every three projects. Higher is better.

2. New booked work per employee measured in net fees should be at least $125,000. Some firms are significantly higher.

3. Target your cost of sales at seven to eight percent of net revenue ($7,000 to $8,000 spent for every $100,000 in new fees produced).

4. Repeat business should be in the range of 65 to 75 percent each year.

5. Track which staff charges time to marketing and what new work is produced as a result (dollars of new fees per

marketing hours spent). On average, principals should produce a minimum of $2 million in new fees each year.

If you set a few clearly understood benchmarks and stick to your strategy, marketing will become second nature.

QUESTIONS

1. How does your firm compare to the benchmarks above?

2. How will you set your targets and track your progress for the coming year?

3. How will you improve your overall marketing results while lowering costs?

MARKETING: SETTING THE PACE

> "A wise man will make more opportunities than he finds."
>
> FRANCIS BACON

Everybody in the firm, from the principals to the support staff, has an important role to play in the marketing process. Mindful that marketing is essentially about making the connection between what you do well and what the marketplace needs done, this means that every interaction or encounter can contribute to those essential connections.

This starts at the front desk with the person who answers the phone and greets visitors. Is he or she courteous and helpful to all callers? Are clients' voices recognized? If the staff is temporarily unavailable—on the phone, at a meeting or out of the office—does the receptionist know how to make sure they are aware of the call as soon as possible? Are staff who make outgoing calls aware of good phone manners? Do they treat everyone they talk to with courtesy and respect? Do they know how to use voice mail effectively? Are messages taken accurately and returned promptly?

And how about your written communications? Are all letters proofread and corrected for spelling and grammar mistakes? Are meeting minutes issued within twenty-four hours? Are memos concise, accurate, and to the point?

28   Remember that every phone call, memo, letter, or voice mail is a brick in the wall of your reputation. Teaching your staff about good business manners—and practicing them conspicuously yourself—are very powerful marketing tools.

Another key to setting a good marketing example is in your personal interactions, both inside and outside the firm. If you get in the habit of treating everyone, especially your own staff, with courtesy and respect, you will reap the rewards in return. Extend this courtesy to everyone in your professional sphere—clients, consultants, and contractors as well as colleagues. Become known as a pleasure to work with, and in return you will attract clients who are also a pleasure to work with.

At every turn, demonstrate curiosity and helpfulness. When you read an article or a book that's of particular interest, circulate it to clients and staff who may benefit. When you return from a conference or a seminar, hold an in-house session to disseminate what you've learned. If you're always on the lookout for new ideas, you'll find more of them. And don't forget the small personal touches—a card or a call on a birthday shows more concern and makes a better connection than a mailing of one thousand holiday cards. Build your own authentic rapport.

What you are saying with this behavior is: you care about your clients and their concerns; you are constantly on the lookout for ideas that may be useful for them. You want them to be successful, because if they are, you'll share in that success. If this becomes part of your office culture, you'll soon become a marketing powerhouse.

1. What is your marketing style?

2. What do your marketing brochures, Web site, and proposals say about your marketing culture?

3. How do you teach your staff about marketing skills?

4. What is your own authentic marketing rapport?

MARKETING: ATTRACTING THE RIGHT CLIENTS

"When schemes are laid in advance, it is surprising how often the circumstances fit in with them."

SIR WILLIAM OSLER

Whrn fishing, you need the right kind of bait. You also have to be in the right spot. So when marketing, learn to go where the clients are, and have something useful to offer them. Ideally, you want to be in contact with clients *before* they need your services, so that when the idea of a project first occurs to them, you'll already be on their radar screen and they'll naturally turn to you for help.

Thus, you must learn to "swim upstream." Get in the habit of seeing yourself as a strategic advisor to your clients. Help them lay the groundwork for the project and establish the parameters of site, program, schedule and budget. Do research on similar projects so that they'll know what to expect in terms of cost and schedule. Become aware of their financing sources. Offer to assist in writing their RFPs if you can. Since the design and construction process is something of a mystery to most clients, become their guide so they'll know what to expect and what to avoid. If they see you as a partner in the process, you're well on your way to getting the job.

When marketing, stay alert for marketing "truffles." Truffles are those tasty little tidbits that are hard to ferret out but make the meal much more appetizing. When discussing a prospective

project with a client, find out where the hard and soft spots are
in the program, schedule, and budget, and then start thinking
of ideas and solutions that will address those issues. Find out
how decision-making actually works in the client's organization so that when the project is underway, approvals can be
obtained with a minimum of fuss. Get your clients to talk about
their dreams—what's really driving this project? What do they
stand to gain (or lose)? And while you're at it, plant a few truffles of your own. Help your clients realize that working with
you will give them an edge.

Bear in mind that most people want to be an architect in
some way, and they'll appreciate the chance to work with
someone who will treat them as a true partner in the design
and construction process. Remember that two imaginations
are better than one, and that dreams and aspirations are powerful motivators. In short, make a friend of your clients, and
become their "co-conspirator." When clients see you as an
extension of themselves, your odds of getting the job will
approach 100 percent.

QUESTIONS

1. How will you "swim upstream"?

2. How will you become a "co-conspirator" with your clients?

3. How will you add strategic value to your client's projects?

MARKETING: SETTING THE TABLE

"It just shows what can be done by taking a little trouble," said Eeyore. "Do you see, Pooh? Do you see, Piglet? Brains first and then hard work."

A.A. MILNE

O nce you've identified a project that you'd really like to get, done the research, and made personal contact with the client, you still have to secure the commission. There are two basic approaches. The first is "process marketing," in which the ultimate decision is made on the basis of pre-defined criteria and often includes RFQs, RFPs, and interviews. In such cases, you are normally competing against three or four other firms, so that all things being equal, your odds of winning are only 20 to 30 percent—not particularly good.

The second method is "network marketing" in which the final decision is made on the basis of personal contact. (This also includes repeat business, which can easily account for 75 percent of your marketing success each year.) Network marketing is much more powerful and effective than process marketing for a very simple reason—all decisions in the selection process, on any job, are ultimately made by people. People hire people, not business cards or brochures. They'll hire who they think will do the best job and who they trust the most. Hence, even process marketing has elements of network marketing embedded within it.

There are several rules of thumb that should govern all your marketing efforts. First, never respond to an RFP that comes in the mail unless you have prior knowledge of the project or a personal connection already established with the client. Generally, it's a waste of your time. Instead, use that RFP to begin establishing a new relationship if you think that client has long-term potential. Secondly, never enter a design competition. It requires an enormous expenditure of time and money, and the odds are not much better than pure chance. Because creating good architecture depends so much on a true process of engagement with the client, entering a design competition is somewhat like proposing marriage after the first date. It's not the best way to establish a long-term relationship.

Third, pay very close attention to how the project will be financed. While it is true that "form follows function," it is equally true that "form follows finance." When you understand where the dollars are really coming from, you'll have an important key to the client's decision-making process. You'll also need to know how to use those dollars to the best effect. If you don't know how a client expects to finance a project, just ask. This will be the first signal to them that you care about their precious resources. Follow up by doing some research and demonstrating that you understand how much similar projects should cost, using reliable data. The message here is that good design embraces not only aesthetics and technology but also finance. By understanding all three, you can produce a better design. It's a very powerful marketing message.

Finally, take the mystery out of marketing. It's really just a people-to-people process, and clients are real people, just like you. Talk to them in terms that they can understand (never say "fenestration" when "window" will do). Be accessible, friendly, and curious. Offer your ideas freely. Promote the message in your firm that marketing—making that essential connection between what you want to do and what the market needs done—is everybody's business. When you do this, your marketing will become a lot more effective (and a lot more fun!).

QUESTIONS

1. How will you become better at "process marketing"?

2. How will you become better at "network marketing"?

3. How will you discover the client's real decision-making process?

4. What are your next actions going to be?

PLAN FOR YOUR MARKETING SUCCESS

> "The objective is constant market regeneration—
> one must embrace every change in the market
> as an opportunity...change and get on with it."
>
> *DESIGNINTELLIGENCE*

Most firms over-invest but under-perform in marketing, and this has a tendency to produce three unfortunate outcomes: Revenues remain stagnant, salaries lag, and profits are significantly limited. Every firm should have marketing training as part of its strategic plan. Each employee should understand firm-wide marketing priorities and responsibilities. Here's how to promote this culture in your firm:

1. **Spend more time with your clients.** More quality personal contacts and more follow-up notes and letters show that you care deeply about the improvement of your client's condition. Aim for at least 12–14 quality contacts per year with each potential client. Each needs to be customized to fit your strategy. The firm message should be: "We are compassionate—we care—we are part of your solution—we never compromise on performance."

2. **Discuss marketing and sales as a regular agenda item at your weekly marketing meetings.** Each member of the firm should report on real contacts. For example, "Last week I

met the following people, I followed up with personal notes on our stationery, I had breakfast meetings with two current clients and two potential clients, and I passed out our new firm brochure at their planning meeting." Understand the human connections and put more energy and enthusiasm into them.

3. **Spend more time researching potential projects and looking for the right fit.** Don't chase every new project. Instead, invest time and energy where there appears to be a good match. This will improve your hit rate substantially. Understand your potential client's business engine, then you can add your own value.

4. **Implement a new simplified time management system.** The system should remind you each day of the marketing priorities with sample tactics and schedule models. For example, "One of our priority values is excellence in marketing. Each day there will be opportunities to market through calls, notes, letters, e-mail, information and research, alliances, lunches and networking." Make no excuses.

5. **Change your existing behavior.** Agree to spend more time on marketing and to be accountable for marketing results, not just marketing activity. Be hard-headed and soft-hearted. Don't just manage—lead your marketing initiatives.

6. **Establishing new marketing habits in the firm is easier for some than for others, but know that marketing is essential to your mission.** Investing in smart marketing is far more effective than throwing money at a problem and hoping for the best.

1. What role will you play in marketing?

2. How will you spend more personal time with clients and potential clients?

3. How will you change existing marketing behavior in the firm?

NURTURING YOUR RAINMAKERS

"I hear: I forget
I see: I remember
I do: I understand"

MAXIM OF DESIGN EDUCATION

Professional firms need "rainmakers," people who can acquire new business for the firm, nurture ongoing client relationships and establish a working environment that is open, healthy and productive. Real rainmakers are hard to find.

We believe that professionals who can bring in work can be more valuable than those who actually do the work, but they are not mutually exclusive. The best combination is talent with a dual set of skills. Rainmaking and design are not necessarily binary opposites. Some leaders can acquire new business as well as deliver good design, and, in fact, in successful small firms this is often a necessity. The skills of the rainmaker are scarce and, thus, more valuable.

A common assumption many firms make is that the future rainmakers are out there "someplace." Often, however, we find that many firms have someone who has the characteristics of a rainmaker but has not had an opportunity to develop the necessary skills. Often, there are future rainmakers within the firm, unnoticed and without a mentor. They are consciously or unconsciously looking for the right time and opportunity. They need nurturing. Remember that you can grow your own rain-makers. Therefore, the first thing a firm should do is to look inside. These "rainmakers in waiting" are often unrecognized and under-appreciated.

What should you look for in a rainmaker?

1. A presence—someone who is noticed and respected (at any level in the organization).
2. A combination of assertiveness and persuasiveness.
3. An ability to communicate and enjoy it.
4. A sincere interest in other people, both inside and outside the firm.
5. An intelligence that is admired but not overbearing.
6. An ability to "multi-task" socially (sometimes called affability).
7. Healthy self-esteem—they don't take rejection personally.

Honey? There's an architect here 'says you bought him on Ebay...?

As hard to find as rainmakers are, they are easy to lose. The key to healthy growth in a professional firm comes through leaders who can be rainmakers but who also understand and nurture the human condition of the firm as a whole.

Keeping rainmakers is a huge responsibility because the health of the firm depends on it. Special compensation frameworks are sometimes advisable. Use not only a competitive base salary but also an incentive system based on both the volume of new business and the total profitability of the firm.

Should you give equity to rainmakers as a part of the total package (i.e. percentage of ownership)? It depends on the culture of the firm and current agreements that are in place. In smaller firms, it's often advisable to give equity positions to keep high performers committed for the long term. In some situations, we recommend a hybrid profit sharing program. An incentive pay-for-performance ratio is sometimes advisable because it works. The principal is simple: when growth and wealth are created for the firm, those responsible should be compensated accordingly. When rainmakers get rich, so too the owners. For the rest of the employees the benefits are also clear——better projects and greater opportunities for professional growth.

1. Who are the potential rainmakers in your firm?

2. How will you train them?

3. How can you use compensation incentives to reward those who produce measurable value?

BUILDING YOUR BRAND IMAGE

"Not a trademark—but a lovemark irrevocably binds you with the desires and aspirations of your clients, your customers, your believers."

KEVIN ROBERTS

In these times, no firm or organization, not even a global titan is safe from the rigors of competition. Economic shifts are everywhere. Dot.com businesses, once the darlings of Wall Street, filed for bankruptcy in droves. Firm consolidations are rampant. The stock market is volatile. Global terrorism and security issues are putting new pressures on the A/E/C industry. Interest rates have sunk below ranges that have historically been seen as normal. Smart firms are strategic in how they respond to such volatility. They can't afford to rest on their success. Other firms could catch up. Clients will move to new value propositions. Firms must continually look for new ways to ensure success. Where are the next opportunities?

Clients want solutions. What clients need most is a trusting relationship with an expert who can provide them. It is rare when a client asks to build a monument to the human spirit. More likely, they are challenged by the task of expanding their facilities, relocating a division, repositioning their business or moving their organization to the next state. Clients know they need an expert who understands the gap between today's operating reality and tomorrow's new business paradigms. They

GRAND BRAND MODEL

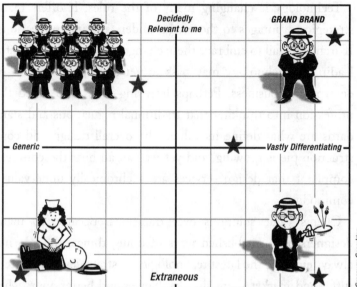

are looking for someone who speaks their language and who is familiar with the unique characteristics of their industry. They not only need an architect, engineer or designer, but also a problem solver who goes beyond typical thinking.

Speed, cost, and performance are the primary drivers. One of the three usually takes precedence. As architects and engineers, we should listen carefully to determine what our clients' priorities truly are and tailor our project delivery systems to meet and exceed those expectations. If speed is the issue, we should streamline the design process without sacrificing quality. The designer who is in tune with the value systems of the client and who understands the primary drivers of the project will become a true collaborator/innovator in partnership with the client.

Technology is changing many of the rules. It offers many strategic advantages to those who understand its implications. If architects fail to embrace these changes, the responsibility for leading in technology may pass to yet another profession or enterprising business. Perhaps licensing laws have lulled the profession into thinking that traditional regulations and standards are what define its value. The overall design and construction pie is growing, and yet we can all hear the common complaint that design services are a chronically undervalued commodity.

Clients value solutions over traditions. Because so many designers have established ways of doing things, they do not always embrace the latest technologies or strategies. Hence, fees suffer and market share shrinks. Newer and better approaches are being sought out by clients. Designers who become more strategic and business-like will become tomorrow's leaders.

Design works in mysterious ways. Celebrate its mystery. Volkswagen made hearts all around the world beat faster when they reintroduced the new Beetle. The clean lines and rounded forms of the design appeal equally to the head and to the heart. Target stores have decided to transform their trademark into a "lovemark." Through cutting-edge design at affordable prices, they strike a balance that makes sparks fly. The Michael Graves product designs for Target now number over 400, each with the power to surprise and enthrall, embracing the "lovemark." And love isn't a one-night stand—it stands the test of time.

1. What is your firm's brand in terms of competencies, styles, and standards?

2. How will you avoid being stuck in the past?

3. What's love got to do with it?

"I used to be the Managing Principal...
I thought the Internet was just a fad."

OPERATIONS: LAYING THE GROUNDWORK FOR SUCCESS

"Operations" is the art of establishing and managing the context within which work can be done efficiently and effectively. Securing space, procuring equipment, hiring the right staff, and crafting office policies are all prerequisites to establishing a productive working environment. Think of operations as "process design." Just like marketing, it is an important part of your overall design process. Without top-quality operations, your talent will be underutilized and underproductive. Setting the right context, like adjusting the thermostat, is one of the most powerful things that you can do to optimize the time, talent, and productivity of your staff.

THE COUNTERINTUITIVE STRATEGIC PLAN

> "Mr. and Mrs. Dursley of number four, Privet Drive, were proud to say that they were perfectly normal, thank you very much. They were the last people you'd expect to be involved in anything strange or mysterious, because they just didn't hold with such nonsense."
>
> J.K. ROWLING, *HARRY POTTER AND THE SORCERER'S STONE*

At a management retreat a thirty-two-year-old designer asked, "Just what do we mean when we talk about the strategic business plan?" She went on to say, "I think that we use strategic plans and business plans as devices to get our attention but then we don't know what to do next." And so began a fascinating discussion that has since changed the performance and profitability of a medium-sized interior design firm into one that was just featured as "best-of-class" in a major business publication.

The young designer's question provided an opportunity to jump start the strategic planning process. After thirty-five minutes of discussion, we had a clear working definition of the term "strategy." We unfolded the definition for the firm, and they made a commitment to provide every employee with a one-page strategic business plan that could be understood.

Here's the working definition of the one-page strategic plan developed at that retreat: *"Our strategic plan determines our purpose, direction, goals and the mission of the firm. It reminds us of the big picture and makes sure that we will spend our valuable resources—our time and money—where they will yield the greatest return. We will express this in one page for every employee to understand."*

Strategic plans need not be mysterious and inaccessible, but instead should be a catalyst for meaningful discussion about the future of the firm. We like the idea of boiling the plan into a one-page document because it provides much needed focus. Here are the key elements:

1. Include the base year plan and the mission statement of the firm in three sentences or less.
2. List targets that will be met in the areas of marketing, operations, professional services and finance. These should be stated in ways that can be measured for each of the next three years.
3. On the bottom half of the page describe the vision of the firm and how the business will be built and managed to achieve that vision.

We recommend that you prepare two versions of your plan. The first is a detailed plan to be used as an internal tool for guiding and managing the business. The second is a one-page strategic summary that can be used to communicate with staff and prospective employees the direction of the firm. It is not surprising that firm principals tell us that the one page version does more good for the firm than the comprehensive model.

Should your staff participate in crafting the plan? Absolutely. Not only will they have good ideas for advancing your firm, they will work harder to support something that they helped to

ONE-PAGE STRATEGIC PLAN SUMMARY

What	*Who*		*When*	

		Year 1	**Year 2**	**Year 3**
MARKETING *Getting the Work*		* Book ____$ in new work * Set budget at 8% of gross revenue * Integrate healthcare marketing * Initiate PR program	* Book ____$ in new work * Set budget at 7% of gross revenue * Maintain a 6 mo. backlog * National publications, articles, & seminars	* Book ____$ in new work * Set budget at 6% of gross revenue * Integrate education marketing * Maintain a 12 mo. backlog
OPERATIONS *Supporting the Team*		* No project losses * Create CAD plan * Create space plan * Reduce OH 5%	* All Projects Profitable * Implement CAD plan * Implement space plan * Reduce OH 5% * Establish parametrics	* All projects run on target * Full CAD operations * Complete space transition * Maintain low overhead * Achieve *super efficiency*
PROFESSIONAL SERVICES *Doing the Work*		* Focus on design * Improve CD process-5% * Use CAD on all projects * Develop LA, ID, STR services	* Win design awards * Improve CD process-10% * 100% CAD literacy * Stand-alone services for select projects	* National design recognition * Top-quality CD accuracy & efficiency * 100% Parametrics * Award-winning LA, ID, STR services
FINANCE *Counting the Money*		* ____% in annual revenue * 8% Profit * Budget & track all projects * Positive cash flow	* ____% in annual revenue * 12% profit * All projects profitable * ESOP plan	* ____% in annual revenue * 20% Profit * All projects at target * Profit sharing plan

Mission Statement Summary _____

_____

_____

_____

Vision Statement _____

_____

_____

_____

Strategic Intent Statement _____

_____

_____

_____

develop. It may be counterintuitive to think a one-page plan can be effective, but often, less is more.

QUESTIONS

1. How does your strategic business plan determine your purpose, direction, goals and mission?

2. Is your plan a catalyst for discussion with all levels of the staff?

3. Do you have two versions of the plan—the first, a one-page adrenalizer and the second, a twenty or so page statement of your business value proposition and your step-by-step plan for success?

4. How will you share your "secret" knowledge?

THE FIRM'S VISION

"Do you care about me? Can I trust you? Are
you committed to the success of our team?
Does our vision ignite your enthusiasm?"

RAFAEL MONEO

I n the best firms, the vision is so energizing that it rallies
the staff to make exciting things happen. We believe that
a vision is not a luxury but a necessity. Without it, design
firms are susceptible to drift and lack of focus. Without vision
there is confusion and often disharmony.

There are many firms with good mission statements that
nevertheless lack a discernible vision. A vision is an understandable, credible, attractive future for your firm, expressed in
simple language. A good vision will remind your staff of what
originally motivated them to choose design as a career (visions
are nothing if they are not motivating). At the end of a long,
hard week, staff should still feel a strong sense of a purpose.

Visions inspire enthusiasm, and they reflect the uniqueness
of the firm. They are attractive because they clarify purpose
and direction. Visions are about change and about new desirable practice models. A vision is not a mission statement. It
is not a reflection of today's reality but is a declaration of the
desirable future condition.

Here are ten warning signs that your firm may be lacking a
clear vision:

1. The firm is not as fun to work in as it once was.

2. There is confusion about purpose and priorities.
3. There is inefficiency.
4. There is resentment toward clients and/or senior management.
5. There is gossip and rumor throughout the culture of the firm.
6. There is absence of shared sense of purpose.
7. There is high turnover of staff.
8. There is unnecessary risk avoidance.
9. There is loss of market position and competitive reputation.
10. There is a lack of trust and respect for principals and officers.

What can be done to turn this around? Leaders in the firm must establish direction and inspire others to buy in. It isn't

"Our firm has lost its vision."

always easy. There are choices to be made that require managing behavior, providing authentic leadership, and exercising keen business judgment. Here is what we recommend:

1. Objectively assess the strengths and weaknesses of your firm.
2. Objectively assess the strengths and weakness of similar firms in your markets.
3. Involve all levels of staff in the visioning process.
4. Involve clients in an outside-in analysis.
5. Explore options and consider contrarian innovation.
6. Don't tear down the present; build on the foundations you have in place.
7. Ask what business you are really in and ask how to build on existing value propositions.
8. Determine the key values and cultural elements of the firm.
9. Make choices.
10. Package the vision for internal and external audiences.
11. Implement the vision through an action plan.

Some design organizations suffer from a cognitive dissonance or disharmony and inconsistency among the organization's attitudes, beliefs, and values and people's actual behavior. If so, the organization is functioning in a wasteful manner. A vision, however, will help create a state of harmony and motivation. When vision is present, so also is adrenaline and creativity.

1. What is your vision?

2. How would your clients describe your vision?

3. How will you implement your firm's vision?

DECREASE WASTE AND INCREASE VALUE

"If an organization is to be transformed, the social architecture should be revamped. New values must replace the old."

THE DESIGN FUTURES COUNCIL

This can be a dangerous time to be a designer. Out moded operating methods and external economic factors are decreasing value and undermining professional competitiveness, while at the same time, higher demands are being placed on staff. These are some questions:

- Will your firm set a new record for gross revenues this year?
- Will your firm set a new benchmark profit this year?
- Will your firm see bad habits and inefficiencies creeping into operations?

There is evidence that the design business is undergoing a revolution. Remember that confronting change with conventional wisdom usually doesn't work (in the same way that antibodies don't work on viruses). So, what are best-of-class firms doing to get ahead of the curve to bring more value to their clients, while at the same time building value in their own firms?

First, they are doing a better job of measuring their own performance. Even though most of us know that success depends on accomplishing the priority work and that investing our time for the greatest return is vitally important, we often don't practice that way. Just what can a principal do to improve old habits and promote better utilization? How can they better focus on changing priorities? These are questions leading architects and designers are confronted with as they realize that their effectiveness is being eroded by the inherent inefficiencies embedded in yesterday's practice paradigms.

A firm should look for answers in the behavior patterns of the staff. We believe productivity can be measured, monitored and improved. Firms that accurately measure appropriate outcomes will bring greater value to clients. For example:

- "Our design business is in the business of change. We constantly monitor the following: 1) What is becoming more important to our clients; 2) What is becoming less important; and 3) How should we allocate our resources differently?"
- "We recognize that the well-managed firm keeps costs and expenses low. Efficiency means reducing expenses that don't contribute, one way or another, to serving our clients. We are lean and fit and committed to resiliency."
- "Our design firm is about serving our clients and producing good design—not just about making money. Profit is our reward for serving our clients well. Profit is the means and measure of our service, but not an end itself."

Honest feedback drives improvements. Firms that use simple scorecards to measure the inputs and outputs—the volume and the value—find that employees will understand how to manage their time better. The firm's culture will take on new and healthier characteristics. Productivity will improve.

Firms that have discovered how to measure and communicate their priorities learn that their success begins to unfold in new ways. They start to aim higher, providing value-added services that improve the client's condition, meet their profit goals and provide the financial strength to grow the firm's value.

QUESTIONS

1. What are five ways to measure effectiveness?

2. What will you do to keep costs and expenses low—to lower your break-even point?

3. What feedback loops will you implement in order to monitor progress?

LIVE YOUR VISION: THE WELL-DESIGNED OFFICE ENVIRONMENT

"Image is everything"

B. JOSEPH PINE II

When it comes to your workspace—your office environment—don't just claim that good design benefits clients. Instead show them what you mean by how you actually live. Your own strategic objectives will be greatly strengthened through practicing what you preach. Use your own life as a demonstration of design ideas, organization methods, anti-clutter, and for high performance. Remember that your firm's office and studio environment actually defines you in the minds of your clients and the world beyond. It's your brand. *You are how you work.*

We have come to understand that there is a significant link between workspace design and top organization performance. Architects, engineers, industrial designers and interior designers are visual people. Yet many do not work in a well designed, well organized, uncluttered environment. Design professionals who work in clutter will confuse the priorities of the day. Organizationally, they can become dysfunctional in a space that is at a glance "in chaos."

One of the key priorities for design firms is to present their office environments as a model to clients, fellow professionals, and future employees. The result will be enhanced productivity, greater satisfaction, and lower turnover. We also encourage colleges and universities of architecture, engineering and design to teach organizational skills and discipline in workplace design and operations strategy.

Consider the prospect of attracting new talent to your firm. What are prospective employees looking for? They are looking for a place to believe in. When we asked architects and designers who were in the process of seeking work to express the values that they were looking for in employment here is what they told us:

1. They want a firm where they can feel appreciated, fairly compensated, and recognized for their true talent.
2. They want to work in a firm where they genuinely like their leaders/mentors and where they feel they can learn and grow as professionals.
3. They want to work in a space where they are reminded of why they chose the design professions in the first place. They want to be proud of the design culture and reputation of the firm.

Take a good look at your own office environment. Now more than ever, architects, engineers, and designers should work in spaces that reflect their values and aspirations. It's not just about what's innovative—it's about what really works. It's not just about what will "wow" people—it's about what people will respect and admire over time. Workspace design matters significantly in the success of the professional firm.

Sometimes firms are so caught up in day-to-day pressures that they fail to take proper care of their own spaces. Clutter develops and the organization slips. Living good design is something we talk about but don't care enough about to live ourselves. In the eye of future employees, to say nothing of clients, these firms are suspect from the start.

In today's business environment, design firms can't afford not to have an attractive, well-functioning workspace. It's one of the bottom-line factors that future employees consider when choosing which firm to join. It's increasingly a factor in client decisions as well. Think of your space as a strategic weapon. Use it wisely. Consider your well-designed workspace an important tool and expect a return on your investment. You won't be disappointed.

QUESTIONS

1. What does your workspace say about you? How do you know?

2. How can your office environment attract new hires and clients?

3. What will you do to create a high performance workplace for your firm?

INFORMATION OVERLOAD: BEAT THE COMMUNICATIONS CRUNCH

"There is nothing more frustrating than a sail-
boat and a crew without an order of events, a
team plan, and leadership."

LYMAN S.A. PERRY

What is the single most important factor in producing a successful project? Contrary to popular
wisdom, it's not great design, or technology, or
management of the budget or schedule. It's communication.
Today's complex projects require large teams of professionals
that include many key stakeholders: clients, consultants, and
contractors. However, all this expertise is of little use unless it
is properly linked up.

Communication is like the gravitational field that keeps the
planets in orbit. Pervasive but invisible, it's what holds the
solar system together. People often complain that there is not
enough communication on a project, but sometimes there can
be too much. Voice mail, e-mail, faxes, cell phones, pagers,
teleconferencing, and the Internet have altered the communications landscape forever. Ironically, the problem is that
there is no longer any conceivable excuse for being out of
touch. Yet, even with all these new ways to "talk" to one
another, there seems to be more confusion than ever. How is

it possible to make sense of information overload and boil it down to simple and effective communication, particularly when so many people are in constant motion?

The core issue is one of "signal vs. noise." Not every fax, phone call or e-mail has the same intrinsic value. Some need immediate attention; others should be ignored entirely. Still others are important but routine, and administrative staff can handle them. Then there are the critical items that can affect the outcome of a project. This is where judgment comes in. Should that phone call from the contractor be returned right away, or will it hold for a few more hours, days or even weeks?

The general rule of thumb is that most problems start small and quickly expand if left unattended. Fix them right away, and they're gone, but ignore them at your peril. The good news is that if the problems are small, they can often be delegated to others. Good communicators know which valves to open and close so that information flows effectively to the right places.

The trick is to get the proper linkage between the sender and the receiver. It's important to remember that hearing is not the same thing as listening, and that talking is not the same as connecting. Only when both the sender and the receiver have arrived at a common understanding has real communication taken place.

Suppose a structural question pops up at a job meeting, and you relay the message to your structural engineer. You assume things get taken care of right away. What you don't realize is that the engineer's voice mail already has ten messages and he won't get your call until the end of the day. The contractor, on the other hand, is looking for an answer immediately and he thinks no one is paying attention.

The contractor sends a fax reminder, copied to the owner, and the owner follows up by calling you. By this time, you're off at another meeting. Now you have a voice mail to respond to, and because the owner is involved, you decide to respond in memo form with copies to all three parties plus the project file. Once the paper trail starts, the contractor feels compelled to ask for additional information, and puts the item on the agenda for next week's project meeting.

By this time, the engineer has gotten the voice mail message and responded to the original question, but only to the contractor. Now another memo is required to reassure everyone that the issue has been satisfactorily put to rest. What started as a five minute question has generated lots of paperwork and more heat than light. The problem has been compounded by the simple but dangerous assumption that access to instant communications means that everyone is instantly informed and instantly responsive. It is not always so.

By the time you have opened your mail, cleared your phone messages, scanned the e-mail, read the overnight faxes and memos and excavated your in-box, you're already buried in information overload. This bombardment of information is changing the very nature of the design process. Design cycles are greatly compressed. Much more information flows to all team members simultaneously, and consequently there is less management hierarchy.

What's the best way to cope with all of this? There are three basic strategies: sorting, prioritizing, and delegating:

1. **Sort.** This means dividing up the workflow into discrete chunks, which is usually done on a project-by-project basis. When information lands on your desk, you need to

know right away where to put it. Some people use multiple in-baskets, one for each project, and this reduces one big pile of work into digestible pieces. For those who are technically inclined, computers can be a great help in sorting the workload. Others prefer to work with paper, and even print out each e-mail so that it can be filed conventionally.

2. **Prioritize.** Obviously, some issues are urgent and demand immediate attention. However, that attention does not always have to come from you. Remember that there are two kinds of priorities: those things that are most important and those things that have to be done first. They are not always the same. When setting priorities, ask yourself who in your organization or project team is the most appropriate person to handle a particular issue, and try to think of someone other than yourself. People outside your own office, including consultants, the contractor and even the client, are fair game. The bigger the group, the more likely it is that someone can get the right answer sooner.

3. **Delegate.** Getting other people to help out is good strategy. It not only reduces your workload, it also creates buy-in for the solution, spreads knowledge throughout the project team, and demonstrates "bench depth" to your clients. Just about anyone in your organization can be a problem solver and handle certain tasks effectively. One of the best ways to get this process started is to use junior staff to double check that the drawings were sent out, the invoices received, or that the client confirmed a meeting. Get people started early in understanding the importance of both accepting and delegating tasks. And remember,

you can delegate authority, but not responsibility. At the end of the day, you are still on the hook for the final results—and this is all the more reason to learn how to be a truly effective delegator.

There are other ways to cope with communications overload. Some people like to get to the office early to get at least one uninterrupted hour per day for maximum productivity. Others prefer to leave early but take the office with them by setting up fax, e-mail, voice mail, computer modem and copying capacity at a home office. This enables work to be done in short, quick bursts when it's more convenient.

Still another technique is to deliberately limit your access. Inform your clients that you are generally available for calls at certain hours of the day, but more difficult to reach at other times. Throw away your beeper. Turn off your cell phone except when you want to receive calls. Ask consultants and contractors to use only fax or e-mail, but not both, and have a secretary carefully screen your calls. Software is now available that will automatically combine all communications channels so that you can better control the flow.

Information overload is here to stay, and that's both good news and bad news. Because it's a relatively new phenomenon, many people have not yet learned how to cope. You might feel like a victim, but you are also a perpetrator. You are receiving much more information than ever before, but you are also sending it out at a record pace. Edit your own communications style to focus on the essentials. Do you really need to copy twenty people on that next e-mail? Do your memos really have to be longer than one page? Do only what you have to do, and delegate the rest. In other words, generate signal, not noise.

The mark of a good communicator is the ability to make maximum impact with minimum fuss. Ultimately, it's not so much the quantity of communication that matters, it's the quality.

QUESTION

1. How will you prioritize messages to make sure the most important get returned first?

2. Are you a good delegator? Would your staff agree?

3. Do you generate more signal than noise?

DESIGNING A PERFORMANCE COMMUNITY

"The root of most conflicts and misunderstandings lies in the absence of communications."

JAMES BARKSDALE

Most firms have an abundant supply of brainpower—yet many do not take advantage of it. New networks of people have insinuated themselves into the culture of design as stealthily as CAD, and these networks create communities that operate both inside and outside the firm. This ultimately affects the success of both the individuals and the firms in which they work. Just as real power is often silent, these networks don't normally show up on organization charts. Yet the nervous systems of the organizations comprehend and behave differently due to their presence. Morale, performance, humor and caring are all connected to the power of these networks.

The perception is that some firms are delivering value and consistent results because of a strong sense of community produced by informal networks that live in the souls of the organizations. Leaders of organizations are then challenged to become more involved in understanding and interweaving their processes and systems with those of the informal networks.

Network power is a significant strategic issue for firms. For example, when there is a sense of community, better people are recruited. Existing employees bring in new talent, and the firm is more magnetic in the way that it attracts people. There is lower turnover and more peer accountability, and there is more facilitation rather than blocking of progress.

Designing a performance community is an achievable goal. One way to get started is to promote a business model in the firm that people understand and respect—including the values and visions of the firm. Here are some steps to enhancing a performance community in your organization:

- Establish strategic clarity in the firm.
- Respect the dignity of all—especially those who need guidance on performance issues.
- Treat all people fairly—nothing reveals the character of leadership more poignantly.
- Be open about financial objectives and performance.
- Measure what you value, because you will become what you measure.

Firms can transcend many common problems experienced in the mainstream of professional service management. What works inside a firm works in the increasingly networked client community as well. This can be achieved through design. Your network power will determine how you keep and attract both the best clients and the best talent to serve those clients.

To optimize your daily performance, break away from old limiting beliefs and habit patterns and:

1. Spend time with people you want to be like. You are likely to become like them.
2. Establish eye contact with and smile frequently at others.
3. Confront and deal with situations involving conflict early on.
4. Don't think in black and white terms.
5. Don't associate with toxic people.

Your role in strengthening your firm will challenge both your *brainpower* and your *actions*. Successful firms are led by people who understand that both are necessary and need to be exercised daily.

QUESTIONS

1. If your staff members were asked to describe your personality, what would they say?

2. How will you develop a sense of community in your firm?

3. How will you improve the social networks in your organization?

HAND-OFFS: DELEGATION BY DESIGN

> "Great design and project achievements invariably involve the cooperation of many minds."
>
> LORD NORMAN FOSTER

In our increasingly complex world, the success of a project hinges on the "choreography" among the owner, designer, engineer, consultant, product manufacturer, and contractor. No single entity has the talent, knowledge, experience or resources to produce a project entirely alone. This means that there is real opportunity for those who know how to get the best out of a group effort, respecting the contributions of individual talents while bending those talents to the overall good of the project.

The one sure way relay teams will lose the race is if the baton is dropped. Many a football game has been blown by an inopportune fumble. And in baseball, a sure out can easily be turned into an unearned run by a bad throw. While it takes talent to produce good results, it also takes teamwork.

How many of us have been in a similar situation? We assume that we understand what is required, and we do our best to make it happen. But somehow things don't turn out the way we expected. Proponents of the Total Quality Management (TQM) movement use the customer and supplier analogy to illustrate how each one of us functions in a team. We depend on others for information to do our part (as customers), and we delegate work to the team (as suppliers) so that they can do theirs. Trouble festers if there is a glitch at either end of the transaction.

A classic example is the transition between CD (construction documents) and CA (construction administration) phases of a project. Many good intentions have gone up in smoke during CA, not to mention profits, because the design and budget are not reconciled or there are insufficient fees remaining to manage the job properly. Ironically, it is only during the CA period that the true quality and value of the designer's work are made manifest, where the project gets translated from mere lines on

paper to real built space. Without good CA, the best design intentions come to naught. This is where the absence of a good hand-off can have a huge impact on the outcome.

The lessons are simple but surprisingly hard to implement. Pay attention to your hand-offs. Be a good "customer" by not accepting hand-offs that are incomplete, confusing or just plain wrong. Be a good supplier by making sure you know what the next person in line is really dealing with and what they need to get the job done.

The role of a project manager, or choreographer, represents real value added to the design process, where the cost of making decisions often goes unrecognized and unappreciated. This is an ideal role for the designer to play.

QUESTIONS

1. What's your delegation style?

2. How will you use your position to help your staff feel valued, encouraged, and linked?

3. How will you teach your staff to delegate properly?

SCALE CAN BE STRATEGIC

> "It is not the strongest of the species that sur-
> vive, nor the most intelligent, but the one most
> responsive to change."
>
> CHARLES DARWIN

Design entrepreneurs understand that growth is a strategic advantage. Why do some principals operate their firms on a month-to-month basis without any urgent desire to grow? Often, they simply don't think of it. We now know that the most successful firms are also growing firms because they planned for growth. Some even make it policy. They do this because they have discovered that size matters.

There are those who say that you need to learn how to grow quickly or you will be overtaken. But more often, we see a different motivation for growth. Growth is a strategic advantage because:

1. It better serves growing clients.
2. It improves shareholder value.
3. It provides opportunities for staff development and career building.
4. It means that there is increased capacity to deliver the goods.

Growth begins as an attitude. In just about every major city today there are firms, many of them first generation or with new leadership, who are like rockets—outpacing the growth of the traditional firms. These new leaders are apostles of growth.

know that growth brings opportunity. They also know that you
cannot grow your own firm unless you also contribute to the
growth of your clients. The value added is an intelligent investment. Growth improves profitability and the balance sheet—
not just the size of staff.

Make growth a policy. Some firms are establishing a market-
centered model of growth. Consider these components:

1. Each market center is established as a profit center. Most
   firms set a 15 percent profit standard.
2. Each market center acts as a central bank of expert knowledge—the most up-to-date storehouse of information and
   facts in their service areas.
3. Each market center is led by an energetic performer who
   knows how to get results and can achieve growth to meet
   the firm's plan.

Growing firms do not just measure size. For them, growth
does not merely mean how large the firm is getting. Growth
can be measured in many ways. One key growth area is in the
quality of project management. Importantly, this also indicates
how consistently profitable that growth is.

QUESTIONS

1. How will you grow to better serve clients, improve shareholder value and provide opportunities for staff development?

2. Your firm cannot grow unless you contribute to the growth of your clients—what are you doing for them?

3. Growth is not just in size. It is multi-dimentional. What is your definition of growth?

4. What is the small firm advantage?

"The best way to get a good idea is to get a lot of ideas."

LINUS PAULING

Perhaps your firm is busy, backlog is up and revenue projections are looking strong. Feeling good? Not so fast! When your biggest problem is finding enough qualified people to staff your projects, you are in the danger zone called "growth."

It might feel terrific to have a long list of clients eager for your attention, but if your growth is not very carefully managed, you are on the verge of big problems. It is ironic but true that firms suffer more long-term damage from poorly managed growth than from lack of work. This is because when work is thin, it is much easier to focus on exactly what needs to be done in order to survive. But when times are flush, problems are easily camouflaged, and they will surprise you at the most unexpected and inopportune times. Remember that the damage done by a project gone sour can last for years.

For many firms, growth is reactive—people don't think about why, how or when to grow until they are overcome by pressing deadlines. Sometimes that long-awaited project that has been on hold finally gets the green light. Sometimes a long-shot RFP hits pay dirt. Sometimes a client decides to increase the scope of work without adjusting the schedule.

One or two new jobs in the office can put unexpected

pressure on your other obligations. The common reaction is to hire more staff as quickly as possible. But don't do anything until you have thought through the strategy, tactics and logistics of managing growth properly.

"Rather than reduce our staff during this downturn, I'm asking each of you to find a void and fill it."

Managing growth is not about putting warm bodies in empty chairs and hoping for the best. Getting bigger as quickly as possible almost always causes a revenue squeeze and quality control problems. First, you have to take time out of your already busy schedule to sort through resumes and check references, conduct interviews, get feedback from your colleagues, structure an offer, confirm an entry date and then arrange the proper support for the new hires.

When the new hire arrives, you are likewise distracted by the usual meeting and greeting, orientation for standard policies and protocols (your CAD layering system is only one among many) and the extra dose of project supervision that it takes to make sure the transition is a smooth one.

Multiply all of this by the number of new staff you need, and you can easily see that when you are in a recruiting blitz, nothing else will get proper attention. On top of all this, the new staff will be collecting a paycheck at least thirty to sixty days before your invoices will be paid by the client, so you are financing all this growth up front. And this is just the beginning.

The good news is that the pressure for growth will force you to think more strategically about your business and the clients that you serve. It will make you reconsider your staffing profile, what kinds of talent you need, who your real contributors are, the nature of your compensation structure and how your firm stacks up against the competition as a desirable place to work.

The very best time to do this thinking is *before* you need new people. This is important for two reasons—it reduces pressure when you really need to concentrate on current deadlines and it impresses your staff as well as the prospective hires, who are now persuaded that you do in fact think and manage ahead of the curve. The truth is that smart firms are always in the recruiting mode, seeking the best-qualified talent, whether or not they are in the hiring mode. There is a world of difference.

When opportunity knocks and you have to hire quickly, what's the best way to go about it?

1. **Be sensitive not only to the short-term pressure for extra staff but to the longer-term implications.** When today's fire drill is over, where will your new staff be assigned next?

This means that to be successful, you need to be resilient, and this means that your marketing program and staffing plan have to be synchronized. So as you hire, make sure that the current growth spurt will be sustainable.

2. **Review and refresh your employee manual, compensation package, office policies and orientation program.** If you don't have an orientation program, create one, and make sure that everyone in the firm goes through it, both recent and longer-term employees. Remember that you want the new staff to hit the ground running, and the key to making this happen is not just the new staff themselves (they are already eager to adapt), but also the existing staff who also have to live with all those new faces. Be aware that there is likely to be some resistance to the new people. It helps to organize social events so that everyone can soak up the corporate culture in a less formal setting.

3. On the logistics side, make sure that your technology is in place to support additional workload. As the firm grows, make sure you have planned for enough phone lines, fax machines, printers, secretarial help and filing space. Are your computers, networks and software licenses up to date? Nothing is worse than getting a new person on board without the tools to be effective from day one, but it happens surprisingly often. Remember that the first day on the job makes a very powerful impression on new staff—your organization and preparation set the tone for their future success.

When you have done all of this, the real job of smart growth is just beginning. New staff need extra coaching. Make time to check in every couple of days to see how things are going. Ask

them what's working well and what still needs some attention.
Listen carefully to their observations about the firm, because these fresh impressions are extremely valuable. Make sure that you take the steps that will support their success, and at the same time stay alert for signs that the fit might not be right. And if it's not right, end the association as soon as possible, despite demanding deadlines.

The single biggest danger from unstructured, unplanned and unmanaged growth is the threat to quality control. It is very easy for new staff to make mistakes—not because they are ignorant or unskilled, but because they are unfamiliar with your system. If mistakes are made, don't compound them by blaming the new people—most likely the fault lies with management who failed to give proper direction in the first place. Be particularly alert to quality control, which is the single biggest risk factor during rapid growth. (The second is protecting your cash flow.)

Your hiring decisions determine your demographics. Since people are the core of your enterprise, you are literally shaping the personality of the organization. The best way to ensure success is to hire with a long-term strategy in mind. Don't just react to today's deadlines or temporary market pressures. Even if you have to move fast, you can still make the right moves.

QUESTIONS

1. How do you manage growth?

2. What is your staffing profile and the types of people you need?

3. How is your growth sustainable?

LEVERAGING GENERATIONAL DIFFERENCES

"The past may be prologue, but which past?"

HENRY HU

The baby boom has had a profound effect on the economy, the environment, and social values. If you manage a design firm today, the odds are pretty good that you are a baby boomer. You have come of age in the most prosperous and technologically advanced generation in history. Until, that is, the arrival of "Generation X."

It should come as no surprise that different generations behave differently. People who grow up in different times, under different influences, develop different values. This is called progress. What one generation takes for context is history to the next.

The differences between generations can be both subtle and profound, including attitudes toward dress, speech, lifestyle, social customs, the work ethic and even music. A lot has been written recently about Generation X, and not all of it is flattering. Adjectives such as lazy, self-absorbed, and greedy have been used, but be cautious about believing everything you read. Instead, deal with your people as people, not as labels.

In managing your design firm, you may notice "chafing" among individuals or groups of different ages. Different personal or educational backgrounds, different levels of experience, and different expectations about compensation all contribute to this. Be alert, but do not be alarmed. Differences of opinion, if properly dealt with, can be very positive for an organization as long as you handle them in a straightforward manner. Diversity can be delightful, and it makes for a stronger firm. However, do not allow diversity to become dissension. Multi-generational, or 3-G firms utilize three generations on project teams to help break down inherent boundaries.

When dealing with generational differences, minimize the negatives and exploit the positives. What is it that attracts people to work at your firm? What gets them excited? What special complementary skills does the firm need to be successful? How can each generation learn from the other? Remember that there are bright and committed people of all ages. Your job as a manager is to clearly communicate the vision and mission of the organization so that all of the staff pull together. This is called leadership.

One firm in the Midwest recently provided an example. This firm had not yet entered the computer age. It was clear that a transition to CAD drafting was needed, but there was considerable resistance from the older generation, who was already proficient on Mylar and not particularly interested in "Nintendo architecture."

The younger staff, however, was energized and excited about using the new technology. Rather than push the changeover from the top down, they let it percolate from the bottom up, and in a very short amount of time, computers and project management software became the standard production tools for everyone. Some of the best teachers were the younger staff, and their enthusiasm was infectious. Today, computers are used by everyone in that firm. But what will the next breakthrough be? Don't you want to get in early—and get ahead?

Remember that each and every generation produces its share of leaders. If you are a baby boomer, the odds are pretty good that at one time you were considered cocky, idealistic, impatient or even weird. Over time, these attributes were transformed to confidence, vision, efficiency and creativity. With your help as a leader and mentor, Generation X, and the generation that will succeed them, will grow and learn. And if you're smart, you'll make a point of learning from them as well.

QUESTIONS

1. How will you deal with your people as people, as opposed to labels?

2. How will you exploit the positives of demographic differences?

3. Multi-generational teams can be very effective. How will you create 3-G teams in your firm?

SUSTAINING GROWTH

"Prophesize as much as you like, but always hedge."

OLIVER WENDELL HOLMES

When times are busy, pressure to grow increases. Like any other dynamic change, growth is tricky, and it requires continual attention. Growth is not just a matter of adding headcount—it's the kind of staff you add and how thay are integrated into the firm that is most important. Growth may be the result of short-term pressure, such as a major new commission with a tight deadline, or it may be due to a strategic shift—adding new markets and services or even acquiring or merging with another firm in order to extend market reach. Either way, there are some fundamentals to be reckoned with.

Growth makes all things different. To most people growth is a sign of success, but it can also produce lots of anxiety, both obvious and latent. (Even changes that most of us would consider to be unalloyed good news, such as winning the lottery, have been shown to create significant stress in the lives of those affected.)

For the newer staff in the office, there will be pressure both to fit in and to stand out. New arrivals will want to make a good first impression and flex their muscles a bit in order to establish their place in the office hierarchy. On the other hand, they will also need to blend in, learn the ropes, find out how things really get done, and figure out the corporate culture and tribal customs of the new firm. If they don't push a little, they will lose the opportunity to make a positive difference in the new firm and may even unwittingly sabotage their chance for subsequent promotion, because first impressions are so powerful. If they stand out too much, there will be resentment from those who have already paid their dues and don't want to see their position in the office pecking order jeopardized.

For the veterans, there is also a dual reaction: relief and added stress. First, of course, is relief that much-needed help is on the way. With new staff, there is more help to get things done and the pressure for overtime will diminish, or at least be more widely distributed. Extra resources mean reassurance; senior management understands the situation and cares enough to take action. At the same time, there is the all too human reaction of "what will this mean for me?" If the new staff is brighter, faster, better trained, or more personable, then conflict can result. Sometimes this conflict is obvious, and sometimes it is subtle. It can be mitigated to a certain degree by lots of communication about who was hired, why they were hired, what they will be expected to contribute, and what kind of help they will need from the existing staff in order to be successful.

This last point is particularly important because the "old timers" are the ones who are usually relied upon to teach the new recruits what is needed and how to get things done. Any problems with transferring this "office DNA" can cause big problems later if standards are not met, or if there is ambiguity or confusion about goals. Thus, it pays to get both sides to understand that they need each other.

The mix of the old and the new in the same organization is

similar in some ways to the physical reactions of orbiting bodies in space. The introduction of any new mass—asteroid, moon or planet—has an immediate and palpable effect on the entire solar system. Gravitationally speaking, each body, whatever its size, shape, speed or orbit, affects all others, even at a great distance. The same effect is true in organizations where the addition of any new staff will have both a local effect and a global effect.

The good news, of course, is that when growth is properly planned for and properly managed, it is sustainable as a state of continuous condition. The firm gains talent, strength, stature, capacity and self-confidence. However, if the effects of growth are ignored, relationships will be altered unexpectedly, and there may even be collisions that cause major disruption. Like real gravity, "organizational gravity" is invisible, but its effects are palpable and everybody feels them in every area of the firm.

As you decide to grow, develop an implementation plan. Ask these essential questions:

- Why are you doing it?
- What specific benefits do you hope to achieve?
- How much will it cost in terms of salaries, overhead, space, and equipment?
- How long will it take?
- How will growth affect the existing staff and existing clients?
- Can growth be sustained beyond the immediate short-term need?
- What will the new staff be doing two or three years down the road?
- How will you measure the progress?

Think of growth management as if you were the dean of admissions at a college whose job it is to compose and balance an entire class of talented and diverse individuals. Since staff is by far the most expensive and most productive asset in any design firm, this is an extremely critical strategic challenge. Don't take it for granted. If you do it right, then you are on your way to an interesting and prosperous future.

QUESTIONS

1. How does growth cause stress as well as relief for your firm?

2. What is your plan to create sustainable growth in your firm?

3. How does your point of view about growth contribute to work/life balance in your firm?

COMPLEXITY AND FIRM SIZE

"Try to value imagination over rationalization."

JAMES STEWART POLSHEK

Increasing the size of your firm used to be a sure signal of success. Staff size is often touted by firm leaders as proof that they are getting stronger and healthier. But is not neccessarily so. Here's why: As organizations grow, they often undergo structural transitions that differ both in kind and degree. Larger organizations often develop new and unantici-pated problems. Sometimes the problems lead to a near col-lapse before a workable leadership structure is put into place. Anthropologist Robin Dunbar of Great Britain has developed a biology-based theory that sheds light on the issue of organi-zational growth. According to Dunbar, functional units larger than about 150 people cannot be effectively managed, nor can their members build critical bonds of support, loyalty and a sense of mutual reliability. Dunbar's work suggests that group size is a key management issue for design managers.

The figure of 150 seems to represent the maximum number of individuals with whom we can have a genuinely social rela-tionship—the kind of relationship that goes with knowing who the people are and how they relate to each other. At Microsoft, Bill Gates keeps business units to a 200-person maximum, a limit he thinks allows most people to know each other by name and allows tracking of their contributions within the accounta-bility structure. Several professional firms that we work with limit their studios to 12 to 15 people. Based on anecdotal experience, here are some recommendations for optimal size, spans of control, and business group performance:

- **Optimum retreat size:** 7. Provides the most effective communication and bonding.
- **Maximum retreat size:** 17. Acceptable levels of communication and bonding are possible.
- **Optimum span of control:** 30. Provides for both individual and group needs.
- **Maximum span of control:** 65. Acceptable individual and group needs are possible.
- **Optimum practice size for team performance:** 15. Provides for an effective performance community.
- **Maximum practice size for team performance:** 240. Acceptable performance community is possible.

Highly capable leaders may stretch the performance of these numbers, but not by much. Functional units of larger than 240 people cannot be effectively managed nor can their members build critical bonds of support, loyalty and a sense of confident mutual reliability.

QUESTIONS

1. What are the right sizes of your teams, studios, and working groups?

2. How do you determine the maximum number of people that can form a team?

3. What size organization is the happiest and most productive for you?

"New blood invigorates a firm and introduces new ideas."

CAL LEWIS

A firm in the South decided that it was time to promote several younger associates. The principals of the firm disagreed on the qualifications for promotion and who should be promoted first. We were called in to listen to the different points of view and to conduct an outside-in analysis of the young talent.

In this instance, the principals agreed that it was time to promote, but they disagreed on who, why and how. This is often the case in growing firms. Regrettably, but not surprisingly, a balanced and critical assessment of talent within firms is among the most poorly performed processes.

When we look at promotion to partner, we look first for leadership. Underlying leadership is respect. In professional firms, respect is earned in various ways. We look for sound decision making, the ability to admit mistakes, assuming accountability in day-to-day behavior, and prioritizing the client's best interest ahead of personal ego or agenda. The Partner Evaluation was developed as a tool to evaluate these and other core strengths of candidates.

LEADERSHIP STRENGTH ASSESSMENT
Partner Evaluation

1. Challenging processes—Continuing improvements

2. Vision clarity—ability to inspire others

3. Systematic priority planning, enabling others to succeed

4. Role model—Stature in field

5. Boosts morale especially during times of stress

6. Builds financial resource strength

7. Communications are at exemplary levels

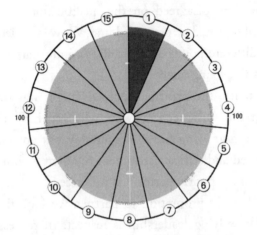

8. Collaborative spirit enriching the people and organizations

9. Steady and strong without alienating egotistic pride

10. Work ethic without micromanagement

11. Applied brilliance—Intellectual power

12. Builds rapport, respect, admiration

13. Custom to Firm's Core Values/Culture

14. Custom to Firm's Core Values/Culture

15. Custom to Firm's Core Values/Culture

©Greenway Consulting

In our story, not one, not two, but three younger associates were evaluated and have now been elevated to new levels of responsibility in the firm. During the process, the older partners earned one another's respect for giving the process thoughtful review. The rest of the staff also better understood how day-to-day choices, behaviors, and character affect both the promotion prospects and actions of the leaders. No leader can break trust with his firm's staff and expect to keep influencing them. Just as in client relationships, trust is the foundation of leadership.

QUESTIONS

1. How do you promote from within?

2. What is your leadership transition plan?

3. Who is respected for true leadership skills in your organization? Why?

DELIVERING BAD NEWS

"Tell them the truth, first because it's the right
thing to do, and second, they'll find out anyway."

PAUL GAVIN

People sometimes find themselves facing unpleasant surprises. And all too often the bad news comes in clusters. It may be a star member of the staff who abruptly leaves, it may be a liability claim that comes out of nowhere, or it may be an unexpected budget problem.

No doubt you have experienced something similar. Budget crises, staffing problems, quality complaints and liability surprises are all too common. Even if it's not your fault, it's on your turf, and it needs somebody to restore direction.

Problems such as these actually give meaning to professional practice today because it is in problem-solving that the true character of people is made apparent. To stay on top of the game, successful firms should anticipate that really bad news most certainly will crop up sometime.

Knowing how to process bad news can become a strategic strength for your organization. When the bad news comes—as it will inevitably—remember that there is an opportunity for you to become associated with the solutions that lie just ahead.

You can set yourself apart from those who insist on acting in ways that tend to reinforce the negatives. When there is bad news, don't attempt to hide it. As quickly as possible face up to the situation and put an affirmative plan into action that informs all the stakeholders. Your message should be lean and forthright about the problems.

Most importantly, you should include a clear plan for what will happen next. Communicating the bad news is a basic professional responsibility, but it is moving forward with options and solutions that is even more important and makes for true professionalism. It is one way of being respected and remembered for seeing beyond the pain of the day to the opportunities of tomorrow.

While bad news may test the character of the firm, it need not weaken the firm or its relationships. How a firm works under pressure in times of crisis will, in fact, define its character.

QUESTIONS

1. How do you deliver bad news?

2. How will you anticipate better?

3. How will you follow through?

LEADING INDICATORS OF ORGANIZATIONAL HEALTH

> *"If we did all the things we are capable of doing, we would literally astonish ourselves."*
>
> THOMAS EDISON

Quality management gurus are fond of saying that in order to improve anything it must first be measured. Measurement requires calibration, and calibration inevitably gives rise to data. However, collecting information and knowing what to do with it are not the same thing.

Often in the design profession we encounter resistance to measuring the creative process by which we produce our work, as if measuring design somehow undercuts its value. Ironically, the opposite is true. It is the very lack of measurement that creates so much confusion in the eyes of our clients about the value of what we do.

How does good design contribute to client success? How is this value produced? How can the design process, and thereby the results, be greatly improved? The answers to these fundamental questions form the basis for creating better design at much higher levels of profitability.

There are numerous software packages that will track key indicators for a project or an entire firm. We are all familiar with the printouts, and they make our eyes glaze over. We can dig deep into details and pull out arcane bits of data, but do we really understand what this data is telling us, and moreover, what to do about it? Probably not, because we often suffer from too much data or data that is poorly organized.

A printout presents a frozen slice of life at a specific point in time. Yet we know that all clients, projects, staff and firms are dynamic in nature and constantly changing. By the time we get our hands on the numbers, it's often too late to fix a problem, or the nature of the problem has changed. We need a way to digest the data without being overwhelmed. What's to be done?

Start by simplifying. Make sure that the "data" you receive is really data, not information contaminated by opinion. (A classic example is the percent complete column on a project printout, which implies a soothing precision that is simply not possible to achieve.) When you have separated fact from opinion, you have taken the first step. Now condense and arrange the information to illustrate not only the status of your operation but also trends. It is possible to do a quick and accurate scan of your firm by looking at only six key indicators:

1. **Monthly billings.** Cash flow is the lifeblood of a design firm, and presumably you are already aware of how much cash is needed to sustain your organization for a typical month's operation. If the accounting department does not send out invoices for at least that amount every month, eventually you'll be in trouble. Therefore, the first and most important number is the dollar amount of monthly billings. While this may ebb and flow a bit, don't let the three-month blended average fall below target. Benchmark target: 8.5 percent of your annual revenue.

2. **Accounts receivable.** Billing your clients is one thing, getting paid is another. A/R measures the average number of days required for collection. Obviously, quicker is better, and there is no cardinal rule that says you have to wait thirty days before billing your jobs. Customize your billing cycles for each individual client so that your invoices can be approved and paid as quickly as possible based on their accounting practices. If your A/R report begins to show increasing numbers, it could signal an unhappy client or an unresolved problem. **Benchmark target: 60 days or better for A/R.**

3. **Staff utilization ratio.** Your staff is your most valuable and expensive asset—make sure it's being used to full advantage. Staff utilization is the ratio of billable hours divided by the total hours for all staff, expressed as a percentage. There will always be some non-billable time for vacation, sick days, holidays, administration and marketing, but you want to keep the utilization ratio as high as possible—it's akin to your batting average. It doesn't hurt to let your staff know how many billable hours you expect them to produce each month. But beware—being busy is not the same thing as being productive. **Benchmark target: 60-65 percent for staff utilization.**

4. **Backlog.** This is your unburned fee—the amount of fee remaining in a project at any given time. Track backlogs for all projects and keep a running total. This will translate pretty well into a staffing projection. If you see a bump in your backlog, you will be in a hiring mode; if you see a dip, you'll either have to increase your marketing effort or downsize. Backlog is the amount of fuel in the tank and

relates directly to the marketing effort. **Benchmark target: 9-12 months of backlog at all times.**

5. **Marketing report.** You can't do the work unless you bring it in first. Therefore, keep track of your "new booked work" every month and measure progress against an annual goal. New booked work comes in two flavors—new projects or additional services on existing projects. Track both. And make sure that the new booked work is real, which means it has a written commitment from the client that the project has been authorized to proceed. As with monthly billings, new booked work is somewhat episodic, so pay attention to the three-month average. And remember that projects are often delayed or canceled so that new booked work is not the same thing as future revenue. **Benchmark target: 8½ percent of annual gross billings each month.**

6. **Profitability.** Profits are essential to a healthy firm, enabling you to acquire the best technology and attract the best people. Structure your organization so that profits are accrued on a monthly basis and log the cumulative total. Think of profit as the first bill that must be paid every month before any other. This technique practically guarantees a black bottom line every year. **Benchmark target: 10-12 percent.**

By keeping track of these six indicators, all of which are quantitative, not qualitative, you'll be able to develop a quick and accurate sense of what's going on in your firm, where the problems are and what needs attention. All this data is readily available from standard financial reports and is easily formatted on a single sheet of paper.

These six data points are like the gauges on a dashboard—

they won't steer the bus for you, but they will enable you to be a much better driver. By developing management techniques that reduce complexity and confusion in your practice—techniques that everyone can understand—you'll free up valuable time for doing the single most important thing you do—top quality design.

QUESTIONS

1. What will you measure and why?

2. How is your data collected? Is it accurate?

3. How will you use the six key indicators? Are there others?

PERFORMANCE-BASED INCENTIVES: MOTIVATING YOUR FIRM

"Create the culture that will give your staff the crucial feeling that they are singly important and making a difference."

JONAS SALK

The closing of each year's books is a good time for strategic thinking about the next year. We find ourselves asking the really tough questions as we look forward to the beginning of the new year. The opportunity for a fresh start finds us returning to one particular question time and again: what's driving our performance?

Many client firms with whom we've worked have expressed their concern about maintaining consistently high standards in terms of the work they produce and the relationships they maintain. The issue of motivating their staffs to continually strive for excellence in these areas is the highest.

There are two fundamentals that when used in tandem will create an energized, highly motivated, and achievement-oriented organization. These foundations are an active code of professional ethics and a well thought out performance-based compensation plan. When instilled and implemented strategically, they will lead most well-managed practices to heightened levels of profitability, productivity, and professional satisfaction.

In an effort to encourage employees to achieve higher levels of performance, many design firms have instituted incentive-based compensation programs. However, nearly a third of firms have reported to us that they are experiencing dissatisfaction with their incentive plans or are uncertain of the affect that the plans actually have on staff and overall organizational performance.

With this in mind, we have devised a checklist of characteristics to be included when devising a program for your firm. Our experience has shown that a key to instituting a successful incentive initiative is to develop a program that is inclusive, motivational, and well-defined.

Although these programs require diligence and focus to develop and administer, they have the potential to be powerful motivators and enhance productivity and profitability. The following are five key components of successful performance based compensation programs:

- Plans that work often pay 15 to 20 percent of base salary.
- Key personnel benefiting from the incentive program usually include principals, department heads, project managers and top management, rather than hourly employees.
- The measurements considered when developing incentive plans include overall firm profitability, the performance of specific profit centers, and individual performance.
- The plan's criteria should be clearly communicated and recognize the top performers in objective ways.
- Winning plans focus on rewarding behavior, outcomes, activities and accomplishments that significantly contribute to the firm's competitive fitness and profitability. The bottom line must be positively impacted by a staff member's contributions (otherwise where will the bonus come from?).

1. What performance-based compensation plan will work in your firm?

2. How will this plan make your firm more profitable?

3. What are you willing to invest in order to create a culture of excellence?

BEWARE "LOS"

"Collaboration is like romance. It can't be routine or predictable."

MICHAEL SHRAGE

W hen a spacecraft returns from orbit, there is about a four-minute period when the buildup of electromagnetic radiation is sufficient to block out all radio contact. During this period, no communication is possible between the spacecraft and ground control. At NASA, this period is officially known as "LOS" or "loss of signal."

A similar kind of LOS occurs between senior management and staff. Whether you realize it or not, most organizations comprise layers of management that too often operate like a caste system. Horizontal communication in any given layer is relatively easy and fluid, but communication either up or down the ladder is not. (Think of an apartment or condo building; it's much more likely that you'll be friendly with a neighbor down the hall than one three floors up.) At the highest level of the firm, all communication with senior management from below is filtered in some important way. Whether this editing is conscious or unconscious, it is ubiquitous. The chief executive almost never gets the straight scoop—he or she gets an edited version that is packaged for personal consumption. "Here is what we want the boss to know" or "here is what we think the boss should know" are the filters. Because the staff sees the boss differently than the boss views himself or herself, the view from the bridge is always a bit foggy, with the consequence that senior management is usually somewhat out of touch with the rank and file.

Obviously, any firm whose synapses are clogged with too much novocaine cannot operate nimbly, effectively, or collaboratively. To combat the phenomenon of LOS, it's very important to establish a "communication culture" that encourages candor. Straight talk, clear thinking, and effectiveness go hand in hand.

One good way to do this is to set up project teams that include staff from several different layers in the organization. Such cross-functional teams are a good way to break down the inherent barriers caused by management hierarchies. Another good tactic is to conduct periodic "360-degree" staff reviews, in which each staff member is reviewed not just by superiors, but subordinates as well. This helps each person understand how they come across to others in the organization, whatever their position in the hierarchy. Still another strategy is to promote from within whenever possible. If the ranks of senior management are substantially filled with those who worked their way up from the trenches, it will be easier to maintain trust in senior management.

Most importantly, the chief executive officer must set the right tone. If the communication style is one of openness and approachability, this will be imitated by the rest of the organization. If, on the other hand, the chief executive is remote, guarded, and hard to read, the rest of the staff will conduct itself accordingly.

When considering your communication style, remember that broadcasting and receiving are not the same thing. Often what we think we say is totally misinterpreted by the audience, despite our good intentions. This is like speaking French to an audience of Germans. No matter how fluent you are, you're bound to be misunderstood. To be a better communicator, it's very important to check with your audience about what they *heard*, not what you said. You'll be amazed at the difference.

As the leader, the burden falls on you to ensure that you are both sending and receiving information in the right way—clearly, succinctly, and accurately. Communication is the neural network of your firm; nothing gets done without it. When you are in a position of power and authority, it's too easy and too seductive to broadcast from your pulpit and assume that you are being listened to and understood (much less followed). It's much tougher, and much more important, to be a good listener. Good listeners attract information and ideas, and good listeners engender trust. Hence, good listeners are influential and more powerful.

All firms and organizations have LOS to some degree. When you are the leader of a firm, you are especially susceptible to its symptoms. To get the best out of your staff, they need to know how to reach you. Give them the means and the methods, and let them surprise you.

1. How does LOS affect your firm?

2. What will you do to reduce your LOS?

3. How will you become a better listener?

"Congratulations. I'm promoting you to project manager. Now, why aren't your people billing more hours?"

PROFESSIONAL SERVICES: BUILDING THE DREAM

Professional services are at the heart of the design mission. This is where your passion and your talent can find their true expression. Don't forget that professional services include integrating the work of your colleagues and consultants. Creating drawings, models, and specifications are merely the tangible products of this most important phase, but they are only instruments of service. The true value of professional services lies in idea generation and problem solving, so never forget that your people are your most important design assets. Create a culture where they can do their best work and let them surprise you with extraordinary results.

VALUE BY DESIGN

"Success rests on distinctive capabilities...What distinguishes each successful design firm is that each has something that their rivals do not."

BILL DYE

To most people, architecture is a building—a place to go, a place to work, a place to live. In this regard, architecture is viewed as a product: the end result of a creative process. For many years, this product-focused thinking has defined the architecture profession and has been the mother's milk upon which many generations of aspiring designers have been raised. Students are taught to draw and make models in anticipation of creating objects that will eventually become buildings.

In school, the pragmatic aspects of program or budget are often ignored, or at least relegated to the back seat. Student work is given to charming flights of fancy, unfettered by practical constraint, and this is not altogether a bad thing. Upon entering the real world of professional practice, however, many newly minted graduates must feel like Gulliver—tied down by the constraints of a thousand gossamer threads. Building codes, zoning restrictions, budget limitations, public design review processes, low fees and "unreasonable" client demands all have an impact on the design process.

This should come as no surprise. After all, school is not real life for designers any more than it is for doctors or lawyers. It takes some time to merge the aspirations of the ivory tower with lessons from day-to-day practice. This collision of idealism and pragmatism often leads to a great deal of angst for architects and their clients, but the frustration is wholly unnecessary. Instead, what is needed is a better appreciation of what architects and engineers do and how they create value for their clients. They provide so many different kinds of services to so many different constituencies that sometimes they have a hard time communicating the value of what they do. Not surprisingly, clients are equally confused.

What is the real value of professional design services? Like quality, the meaning of value might seem slippery and elusive, but it needn't be. One simple definition is that value is cost divided by benefit. How much do you pay for something, and what do you get in return? Was it worth the price? That is the essential measure of value.

Let's take a simple example, such as a commission for a new office building. Perhaps the client is a developer whose primary interest is in erecting a structure, securing leases and then reselling the project to an owner with a longer-term financial interest, such as a pension fund. To be a success, the first criterion is that the project must provide a reasonable return on investment, otherwise it simply won't be built. When the commission is awarded, the specific users are probably unknown because the leases have yet to be signed, but the owner knows that the building must appeal to the market. Clearly, controlling capital cost is an issue, as are the interests of various "stakeholders" such as public review agencies that will have jurisdiction over the project.

How does the architect create value in this situation? The

answer includes, but goes way beyond, the aesthetics of the project. Creating value means that the architect can show the owner how to get the most efficient use of the site—maximizing the floor area ratio and the parking and overcoming inherent difficulties such as unusual soil conditions or zoning restrictions.

"Oh, I see you've decided against the glass celings."

Design value also means that the appearance of the building will attract potential tenants and in turn their staff and customers. It should be a place that people will want to come to and work in, with a floor plan that will be easily marketed and leased. It may even attract premium rents by virtue of its design. Value also means that the building materials will be chosen not only for appearance, color and texture, but also for durability. Smart owners know that it costs far more to maintain a building over its useful life than it does to build it in the first place.

Value means providing for flexibility. Since the architect doesn't know who will actually occupy the building, the design must accommodate a variety of potential users, some of whom will have very different and changing needs. The architect can also provide value by helping secure permits and other necessary public approvals.

Value can also be measured by managing the construction cost and schedule. After all, time is money, and the client has an investment interest to protect. Can the project be brought on line at or below prevailing rates for construction cost? Can it be delivered earlier than expected, accelerating cash flow? Doing this creates real measurable value for the client.

Could the architect assist with graphics and signage, creating the marketing image for the building or even, through business contacts, arrange for the client to meet prospective tenants? How about arranging for publicity? All of these aspects reinforce the architect's goal of providing value as part of the design process. It should be readily apparent from this simple example that the designer's potential value to a client is as much strategic as aesthetic.

To be truly effective, architects, engineers, and designers must understand and communicate how their services can create value for the client. When measured this way, the design fee becomes a non-issue, because value (cost divided by benefit) always exceeds the cost.

118 In fact, good design *always* creates value in excess of cost—otherwise, why do it? A good design decision adds value for many years, and a bad one hurts for just as long. Top-quality design skills should be highly leveraged. Architects who fail to understand this principle risk becoming low-cost providers of a commodity service.

By virtue of your design skill, show your clients how you can create more value in all aspects of their projects. This means reconceptualizing professional practice from "product based" to "process based" and "outcome based." Architects are not just providers of design documentation, they are navigators who help clients achieve their goals. Drawing and specifications are instruments of service, but they are not the essence of the service itself. In other words, don't just draw the lines, draw the conclusions.

QUESTIONS

1. How will you communicate a project's value to your clients?

2. How can you show clients that you can create value in all aspects of the project?

3. What distinguishes your firm from others?

HYPERTRACK: SETTING NEW STANDARDS FOR CLIENT SERVICE

"Success comes in thinking toward 'new and improved'—and then creating it."

APRIL THORNTON

The economy has spawned a number of new firms that can compete for work without high overhead. Technology has made the production of sophisticated drawings faster and cheaper. Even high-profile commissions often include some measure of price competition. Talented staff is harder to find and more expensive to recruit. Each of these factors puts a lot of pressure on fee structures and overall profitability. In short, when the market is hot, so is the competition, and when the market is slow, sharpening your business skills is essential to survival.

Smart firms are not waiting for owners to offer higher fees. Instead, they are busy thinking up new ways to serve their clients that will enable them to increase profits even as fees are going down. While this may seem counterintuitive, the truth is that it is not only possible, it is necessary. After all, clients themselves are under similar pressures—they are expected to produce higher quality products and services faster and cheaper all the time. Thus, they are relying on their design consultants not only to keep pace, but to lead the way with new ideas about how to do it. Understanding how competitive pressures affect your client's business as well as your own is a key to becoming a leader in the new economy.

To stay competitive and therefore valuable, throw out all of your old assumptions about how you "should" do business. Think unexpected, contrary and outrageous thoughts. Align your organization with your client's interests first, forming a new kind of "virtual partnership" that can accomplish amazing things by breaking down traditional client/architect barriers. Perhaps most importantly, allow yourself to be pleasantly surprised by the creativity and productivity from every member of your team, no matter what their role or responsibility.

Here's an example to illustrate the point. A design firm in Massachusetts was engaged by a large biotechnology firm that owned a parcel of land. The company was unsure about how to put this property to best use—should it be sold for a profit, developed, leased or land-banked? In the course of the analysis, the design firm became aware of a local down-zoning petition that proposed to reduce allowable FAR (floor area ratio) by nearly 40 percent, greatly affecting the asset value.

This was an important wakeup call. The client needed to decide very quickly about the highest and best use of the property or risk losing more than $30 million in asset value. Naturally, this got the immediate attention of the client's senior management.

Even though the owner did not know what kind of project, if any, made sense on the site, or whether or not they would ultimately occupy a new building for their own purposes, it was clear that being passive was the worst possible strategy. A special project team was formed that could quickly explore a variety of alternatives and take action.

The team included geotechnical engineers, MEP engineers, structural engineers, legal counsel, construction management and real estate advisors. The client chose the architect to manage all the consultants. Communications were immediately set up with key personnel at city hall, and since the client's business was based in another state, great care was taken to make sure that strict protocols were followed in the submission of all materials for review and approval by city agencies.

One of the most pressing goals was the need to submit a "permit set" of construction drawings and specifications as soon as possible for a building that had no program, no budget, and no design. When the client gave formal approval to proceed for this filing, the deadline was less than thirty days away. In just three and a half weeks, a comprehensive set of shell-and-core documents for a speculative $100 million project was completed and submitted to the city for detailed review. The project was designed completely "by right" and was carefully fit on an unusual trapezoidal site that had almost no street frontage.

The schedule and the design challenge both seemed impossible at first, and this required a new way of organizing the effort. Weekly coordination meetings were held, special subcommittees were set up to explore specific issues in detail, and each member of the team was given a clear role and responsibility. Decisions were delegated freely, made quickly and confirmed at the weekly coordination meetings.

Even though the effort was intense, there was no need for frantic amounts of overtime. In fact, the architects and engineers finished the drawings early, enabling them to take a long lunch and still beat the 5:00 printing deadline. This unusual process, which was dubbed "Hypertrack," worked for a number of reasons:

1. **The client committed a full-time project leader who took an apartment across the street from the architect's office and was available to make decisions on the spot as needed.** In addition, the owner committed a number of his own in-house experts to process information quickly and provide instant feedback.

2. **The design firm provided office space on its own premises for the client's team leader, installed special phone lines and assigned dedicated administrative staff to the project.** The firm also provided a clearinghouse for all information and scheduling, issuing meeting notes within twenty-four hours so that everyone was continually up-to-date.

3. **To get things done quickly, it was important to provide "frictionless paperwork."** Communication was done via e-mail, and drawings were posted on a project Web site for easy access, downloading, and transmittal of revisions. Documents were instantly accessible from any location, including the owner's out-of-state headquarters.

4. **The business arrangements were kept exceedingly simple.** All of the consultants were paid on an hourly basis with a built-in profit margin and a guaranteed thirty day turn-around on the invoices. This enabled the team to focus on the job at hand rather than how to get paid or how to manage time to meet a budget. Consequently, what had to get done got done quickly, since staff could be assigned as needed. Ultimately, the cost of the construction documents was about 20 percent less than traditional benchmarks would have predicted, so the client received excellent value for the money.

5. **A lot of attention was paid to getting the right team on the job.** Consultants were selected not only for their profes-

sional expertise but for their cooperative attitude and the ability to commit high-level decision-makers whenever needed. Team morale was kept high by providing lunches and snacks for in-house meetings. There were also occasional dinners out and outings to baseball games and harbor cruises. This helped develop personal trust at all levels of the team.

The lessons learned from this adventure are several. The design team was able to see things through the eyes of the client. They knew which issues were truly critical and how they could contribute their specific expertise to create solutions. Each task was approached from a perspective of "how are we going to work together to get this done?" versus "how did we do this the last time?" Team members at all levels were made to feel important because they were important. In fact, some of the most creative and productive ideas came from less experienced technical staff. And, while the project required a lot of hard work, it was also fun.

The upshot was that the owner was able to proceed with the project in record time and at much lower cost. Speed proved to be an enormous strategic advantage because each month of schedule acceleration was worth $1 million in revenue flow to the project when completed. The process proved to be so successful that certain aspects of it are being studied for adoption as corporate-wide policy. None of this would have been possible if the owner and the design team had been intimidated by the constraints of past practice. What does this example mean for your firm and how you do business?

1. Know your clients exceedingly well—their goals, their resources and their pressures. What are they really trying to accomplish and why?

2. Keep your focus on results and do only what has to be done. Avoid the temptation to be side-tracked.

3. Use your total team resources to devise a new kind of process—figure out where the barriers in the system are and then remove them.

4. Understand that time is money, and know when to spend lots of it in order to generate even greater savings.

5. Focus on flexibility—make the decisions that you need to make in order to move the project forward, but be ready to change at a moment's notice.

By aligning your corporate culture with that of your client, you can redesign the design process. In doing so, even in a competitive market, you will have no competition.

QUESTIONS

1. How will you redesign your work process?

2. How can you make speed an asset rather than a liability?

3. What are you doing now that should be done differently or not at all?

HOW TECHNOLOGY IS
REDESIGNING DESIGN

"A variety of technologies will disrupt many of today's firms and create tomorrow's great organizations."

CLAYTON CHRISTENSEN

When new tools and technologies are applied to a time-honored process, everything changes. When the steam engine was invented, the concept of work was dramatically altered. When automobiles replaced horses, our ideas about time and distance were never the same. With the advent of television, the world shrunk to the size of a global village. Sometimes change is obvious and sometimes it is subtle, but it always has a profound effect.

For example, word processing (what we used to call typing) has quickly evolved from a novelty into a largely intuitive way of creating and filing documents. This has changed the way we write and even the way we think. While some people may still prefer to do correspondence by hand, no contemporary office would or could operate without word processing as a basic technology, and it's fundamentally changed business practices.

The impact of CAD technology on the design process has had a similar effect. Just twenty years ago, when "Pong" was the most advanced video game you could buy, there were dozens of versions of CAD software, many of them requiring mainframe computers. There were no industry-wide standards, and pen

126 plotters (which always seemed to run dry at the most inopportune moment) were the only way to print.

In just a few years, there has been a profound and permanent change brought about by the use of computers as design tools. PCs rather than mainframes are now the norm, plotting is done electronically and in hundreds of colors, industry standards and drafting protocols have emerged, and most clients are not only expecting but demanding that all work be done on CAD. This has affected not only the way we produce design, but also the very way we think about it.

When a new technology emerges and then dominates a time-honored process, both the process and the product are changed forever. In a very real sense, process is product. Those who have embraced CAD enthusiastically and understand its implications are remaking their practices. They are marketing differently, designing differently, managing differently and making more money in the process.

With the advent of e-commerce, limitless possibilities are being revealed. Just like the changes brought about by steam engines, cars and television, the Internet has recast all of our fundamental assumptions about time, space and communication. There are five aspects of this seismic shift in both process and product that are reshaping how design is done:

1. **Image quality.** In the past, architectural drawings were relatively abstract, collapsing three-dimensional information into two dimensions. Plans, sections and elevations were all required to illustrate design ideas. Now, CAD systems can easily work in three dimensions and can add elements of color, shadow, texture and even animation or sound to the "drawings." The drawings themselves are really miniature

"cyberplaces" defined by bits and bytes. Nothing is "real" about CAD drawings displayed on a screen or contained on discs, yet they are much more realistic than anything done by hand.

2. **Speed.** Internet and CAD systems allow faster drafting, speedier revisions and quicker printing than conventional drafting systems. This is a tremendous advantage because it enables designers to consider many more alternatives at less cost, improving overall quality in the process.

3. **Accuracy.** For area calculations, materials take-off, engineering calculations, dimensional coordination and the like, CAD systems have forever altered industry expectations about accuracy. Precision is now a presumption.

4. **Complex Visualization.** Forty years ago, Saarinen's TWA terminal building in New York was audacious and breathtaking with its compound curves. With CAD, such a design could be generated, engineered and tested with relative ease. Since the software for this complex visualization originated in the aerospace and entertainment industries, we also see a blurring of professional boundaries. Is the future of design rooted in art, entertainment, or technology? The answer, of course, is all three.

5. **Design Quality.** Internet technology provides an entirely new way of making architecture. Clients, no longer alienated and confused by old-fashioned abstract working drawings, are able to be much more active participants in making design decisions. Public review processes are the norm rather than the exception. By using CAD systems, designers can communicate with clients and the public much more clearly and convincingly than ever before, and

there is a direct and palpable effect on overall design out-come.

Architects and engineers may still believe they are in the business of designing buildings, but with technology they are doing it in very different ways. In a sense, the process of design has been "microwaved." When you make popcorn, do you get out the pan, heat the oil, pop the corn, melt the butter, and then clean up? Or do you toss a packet of microwave popcorn in the microwave for three minutes and enjoy the same product faster, better, and cheaper?

In a similar way, technology returned the essence of the design process—and its impact is just beginning to be felt. In the future, designers will have entirely new ways of creating and communicating design ideas to their clients, contractors, and the public. Smart design firms are pushing this technology to its limits. They are redesigning what design can do.

In fact, computers may enable us to invent a whole new language of "spatial notation," much like sheet music. With only a few abstract symbols, it is possible to "write" music on paper (a two-dimensional medium) that captures and communicates ideas of melody and rhythm. Musical notation is simple, comprehensive and elegant—and it can be understood universally by musicians playing any instrument anywhere in the world. Complex symphonies or operas, requiring dozens of players with different kinds of instruments ("tools"), can be accurately reproduced using only a few sheets of paper, and still permit a great degree of artistic freedom.

Why haven't the design professions developed such a language? It should be possible to describe space, color, texture, and construction details with equal poetry and clarity. With such a language, the way we go about "doing design" will be faster, cheaper, better and more imaginative. The demands of our clients and the public will make it necessary. The power of technology will make it possible.

QUESTIONS

1. How is technology changing your organization?

2. How will technology change your design process?

3. What resource and staffing changes will you make to stay technically current?

ROI—"RETURN ON INNOVATION"

"We have as much to learn from our imaginations as from past experience."

JONAS SALK

O ne of the lessons we have learned from studying successful firms is that these smart organizations are making a sharp break with old habits, deliberately adopting new ways of behaving. The design organization is a complex socio-technical system whose ability to thrive depends on economic and strategic action. For several decades, there has been a steady increase of complex demands placed on design organizations and will be even more pronounced in the coming years. *With change comes choice.* It takes both courage and intellectual honesty—not only talent—to look at the world anew.

Here are several trends that are remaking design, which are already underway and are likely to accelerate within the next eight years (some much sooner). Think about these issues as they relate to your own organization.

1. **Digital innovations will provide new communication solutions.** PCs, personal assistants, monitors, and computers that will recognize speech. The implications of this development on communications, productivity, intergenerational understandings, and client relations are profound. There will be wearable computers used

on construction sites.

2. **Design-build will occur in more than 55 percent of projects.** There is no doubt now that this is a growing and satisfying service delivery option for clients seeking a single point of responsibility and accountability. The Design Futures Council projects that design-build could grow to 70 percent and become the dominant delivery system.

3. **Changes in zoning laws will encourage mixed-use streetscapes and clustered communities.** We see stores, schools, cafes, and service centers all mixed together closely with residences, in pursuit of a better "sense of community," for reasons that are driven by security, environment, and transportation concerns.

4. **Nanotechnology will exlode.** Not just in smaller chips, but in sophisticated robots on construction sites, in office tools, and even in clothing that contains built-in computers and heat tubes, which could make thin jackets the preferred option for construction workers, skiers, and travelers. Get ready for "smart dust."

5. **Health care professionals, management consultants, and technology professionals will threaten/change the design professions.** As competition and compensation soar in the technology fields and health care, these will become the fastest growing professions in the next five years. Salaries will be higher, attracting talent away from traditional design professions. Some management consultants will expand services and further blur traditional service delivery boundaries, taking more market share.

6. **Recognition will be given to "knowledge entrepreneurs"**

as the solution providers of the future. Those who hold production jobs will increasingly move to the lower levels of the food chain and become less influential. Drafting and CAD operations could phase out or be replaced by outsourced foreign labor.

7. **China, at 9 percent GNP growth, will be not only the largest population but also the world's largest economy.** English will become the dominant language in design and construction projects, as it has in aviation. This will include China as well. China will also become the world's largest design marketplace. They will increasingly export design talent and services and become a global competitor in production.

8. **More than 6,000 new schools will be constructed in the next 5 years and more than 18,000 in the next 10 years in the United States alone.** There will also be major additions and remodeling projects making public and private education one of the hottest markets in the next decade.

9. **Great design firms will become "data central."** Architects can be repositories for facility management documentation, restoration, renovation, and maintenance. Highly advanced data centers will become critical hubs for architecture, engineering, and interior design decisions. Design firms can become the central source for facility knowledge management.

10. **Large organizations will be increasingly vulnerable to the Internet and smaller fast moving solution providers.** Fifty percent of all goods and services will be sold electronically. Unforeseen massive changes or "strategic inflection points" (SIP) can undermine past successes.

These SIPs are potentially positive forces and can also be
used to win in the marketplace and emerge stronger than
ever.

11. **Renewable energy sources like wind, solar, and fuel cells will become cost efficient.** We're all familiar with the smaller-scale satellite dishes used for TV reception. Now, technical advances are taking place in the energy field that will make wind energy a viable choice for a variety of residential and commercial building types. Wind farms will supplant some corn fields.

12. **Aroma will be a commonly used design technique.** Sweeter smelling city streets will lower crime using the scents of coffee and cookies. Offices, airports, shopping centers and health care centers will all benefit from air quality and "scent design."

13. **Illumination balloons/portable suns will aid in nighttime construction projects.** This will allow for quicker turn-around and more control and will be applicable for road construction, building projects and commercial applications.

14. **Increasingly, cities will operate 24 hours a day.** There is an efficiency consideration and a service motivation for cities that will follow the Las Vegas, New York City, Miami, and Paris models. There will be better use of time, energy, and resources.

15. **The "information glut" will be a factor in design communications.** Truly useful information will be easily blurred, buried, and lost. Organizations that differentiate themselves and use the latest technology and Internet organizing systems will be winners.

16. **There will be mega-growth in hotels and resorts.** In the oceans there will be larger cruise ships and man-made islands. There are companies now planning space station resorts—permanent entertainment and casino centers in space within the next 20 years. Hospitality and entertainment design will be in high demand through 2008.

17. **Green and sustainable design solutions will be mainstream.** Hydrogen energy-fission power will be a safe and economical option. There will be an effort to reinvent energy efficiency as the "green movement" advances well beyond twentieth century initiatives. Electric cars or electric-combustion hybrids will be in the majority by 2010. Seventy-five percent of waste will be recycled.

18. **Terrorism and security issues will become key considerations in urban design, product design, process design, and building design.** Experts and facilitators of design systems will be in great demand along with "feeling safe" design.

19. **There will be 100 percent electronic banking.** All taxes will be filed electronically. Invoices will be e-mailed, and corporations will pay fees via electronic banking. Smart cards will substitute for cash. Accountability and security will be much improved. Projects, both large and small, will have their own Web sites for accurate communications, delegations, and timely business transactions.

20. **Material composites will replace traditional metals in buildings.** Ceramic buildings will gain popularity as sand is cheap and easily recycled. Recycled materials will be the majority of the structure in new bridges, docks and buildings. Plastics also have great potential.

21. **Commercial and institutional environments will increasingly become part of the "edutainment" or "experience economy."** Shopping centers, children's hospitals, schools and offices will become spaces that make people feel good and elevate the human spirit.

22. **PCs will include interactive TVs.** This technology is already available, and prices will drop substantially in the next few years. Each PC will have a camera and will enable better communication in and out of the office. Computerized self-care in medicine will become commonplace, including dialogues via PCs where medical professionals can examine and diagnose patients online. Design firms will be able to communicate and establish dialog globally, allowing for greater efficiency and better understanding.

23. **The skills of innovation and optimism will be the most highly sought after by corporations.** Due to rapid changes and evolutionary considerations, the characteristics of agility and optimistic problem solving will be a prime attribute in the new millennium. Intelligence combined with an attitude of optimism and invention will be highly attractive to employers and clients alike.

The Greenway Group consultants keep a daily chronicle of new, emerging, and advancing trends and study of "future potentials" that will reshape the design professions. Of course, there could be unforeseen factors that shift priorities or delay the pace of change. You should always be ready for surprises, disruptions, and accidental events. Professional intervention and resiliency are always the most important skills. You can take responsibility for generating new concepts, identifying enhanced choices, thinking about different scenarios, and how to bring wisdom to the moment—that's the most sought after change of all.

QUESTIONS

1. What future changes could disrupt your firm?

2. How will you be resilient and anticipatory in the face of change?

3. What things must happen for you to be what you want to be?

"Differences can be creative...find ways to allow
people to express their innate talents, rather than
prove their compliance to a firm or cultural norm."

DESIGNINTELLIGENCE

We have experienced some practical new insights about a mysterious subject—the decision-thinking processes of the human mind and design teams. A decision is a judgment. When designers choose among alternatives, it is rarely between right and wrong. Yet those decisions affect outcomes in significant ways. A small difference in a choice can make a big difference in the ultimate outcome. This is what is meant when people talk about life being a game of inches. The stakes are high when these decisions are small ones—much more so than is often recognized.

Historically, design organizations have operated in silos. They separate functions, looking for laser precision and focus, and, in this, they often separate processes. Job descriptions are written in ways that narrow, rather than expand, a person's role.

These well-intended, refined job descriptions anchor people and the teams they affect. They are often not good for much except to reinforce and recognize experience, and they almost always miss the big picture. "That's not my job," is a common refrain, but what is not understood is that this frame of reference is self-centered and ultimately leads to a hardening of the organization's arteries.

138   Redefined design teams are being put in place in many leading firms. For instance, some firms are bringing product experts from the manufacturers right into the firm on a 24/7 basis. A healthcare design firm has brought in a retired doctor and hospital administrator. An industrial design firm has brought in an industrial psychologist. All are key members of the redefined design teams.

Your motivation to bring the power of design to each project will expand your definition of the design profession. Your reward will be in stockholder value, repeat business, and return on investment.

QUESTIONS

1. How do you define design teams in your firm?

2. What changes will you make in order to enhance collaboration?

3. How will integrating other professionals further strengthen your own design teams?

4. How will you integrate all the design disciplines to better service clients?

> "To own the future…businesses and individuals
> alike need to avoid the activity traps that can
> lock them into the present."
>
> WATTS WACKER

One of the biggest problems with maintaining project profitability is keeping each phase of work on schedule and within budget. There is a great temptation to design until you "get it right," even if this means using up fees earmarked for subsequent phases.

Continual design refinements made during the construction document (CD) and construction administration (CA) phases are common and always take more time than anticipated. Subsequent pressure to get out to bid as soon as possible often results in incomplete or poorly coordinated documents. This puts pressure on construction administration—a traditional money-loser for most firms. Throughout the process, designers and managers are often at odds—each one wants to drive the bus and neither wants to be a passenger.

The key to solving this problem is understanding that regardless of where they sit, everybody is riding the same bus. Design is a process that starts with marketing, and does not end until the ribbon is cut at the building opening. A successful project requires more skills than any single individual can provide, including marketing, management, design and technology, as well as financial and political savvy.

If your office is divided into tribes of designers, managers and technicians, each of whom owns a piece of the process in sequence, then you have unwittingly created a culture that will always be at odds with itself. While each aspect of the process is critical, it is the blend and balance among them that determines ultimate success.

The key to getting it right is to create mutually dependent stakeholders. Designers are totally beholden to marketers—they have nothing to do until a project is landed. They are equally beholden to the technicians and the construction administrators who see to it that the lines on paper they so carefully draw can be properly built. Likewise, technicians and construction administrators depend on design vision to guide their work. No one can function without the accounting staff who send the bills, collect the money and write the checks.

If anyone commandeers more than their share of resources — time, money or staff—an imbalance occurs, and it is an absolute certainty that the project will suffer in some important way. There are two important aspects to getting it right. The first is to communicate clearly about what you expect of others on the team. The second part is to understand what they expect of you.

You cannot have a successful project unless all your team members deliver the goods together. This means that if you don't hold up your end of the bargain, everyone else pays the price. For example, if a designer persists in making changes long after design development has been approved, it is very likely that there will be problems with the construction documents, shop drawings or changes in the field. Ultimately, the only way to make sure that a project will be properly carried out is to provide enough time during construction administration to get it right.

What about the notion that you can just take cost overruns out of the profit? After all, isn't it better to spend a little more to get great design, even if profitability suffers? While at first glance this is a beguiling notion, it is a siren song. Running a loss on a project is an extremely expensive tax on your future. Smart organizations understand that healthy profits are the only way to ensure that the design mission of the firm and the project can both succeed. There can be no room in the corporate culture for design vs. management. Instead, you must promote the firm-wide value that design and management are not only mutually dependent, they are mutually necessary. Design is a process of employing resources (time, talent, money) to create a deliberate and desirable result. So is management.

This balancing of design and management issues requires a great deal of discipline. Great design starts in the marketing phase; blossoms as the team juggles the constraints of program, budget, site, and schedule with practical and aesthetic issues; and continues when these fertile ideas are condensed and then frozen into the single option chosen from among the many. Design matures during the construction phase, when ideas on paper find life in real built space. By viewing all of these phases as part of the design continuum, you can provide your staff with a framework with which to understand their respective roles and responsibilities.

It's ironic but true that great buildings, like great art, have more to do with knowing when to stop than how to start. What would have happened to the Pieta if Michelangelo had spent another month on it? What happens to a cake if you don't take it out of the oven on time? In school, budding young designers are encouraged to explore as many options and alternatives as possible. But in professional practice, the best design comes from the wisdom of knowing how to choose the one option among many that should actually be built, and then concentrate on making it work.

Once this choice is made, it must be executed with a great deal of focus and confidence. This requires both the discipline and the generosity to make sure that all phases of the work have the resources of time and talent required for success.

QUESTIONS

1. Explain how design and management are both part of the creative process in your organization.

2. How will you break the habitual patterns of inefficiency in the design process?

3. How will your firm design both faster and better?

BLURRING BOUNDARIES

"An idea can turn to dust or magic, depending on the talent that rubs against it."

BILL BERNBACH

D o you think of yourself as a design manager? An interior designer? A design engineer? Do employees think of themselves in traditional ways that relate solely to their education or their state registration certificate? According to our research with the thought leaders in the industry, if designers don't redefine their job descriptions and expand their view of their professions, they may destroy the very profession they are trying to protect. The good news is that you don't have to destroy your firm to save it. Progress comes not from perfecting yourself along the historical definitions of your profession, but rather from the courage to experiment and change.

There is a blurring of boundaries in design that will no doubt accelerate in the future. This is also true among other professions, such as management consulting, advertising, and real estate. There is a story about a client who approached an architectural firm to help solve a complex strategic problem. A design problem yes—but it was also about branding, global facility design, and the development of a better business model. The firm, a diversified architectural firm, had not been asked to provide this specific service in the past. However, its track record with this client was strong and its stock was high.

The client needed innovative problem solvers and didn't care to turn elsewhere for solutions. This category of service wasn't mentioned in the firm's marketing literature, but, in the client's eyes, they were a stand-out innovator.

This client had a service gap to fill. The architect and his staff went to work imagining how they might fill that gap to provide the best solutions for the client. They looked again at what they thought their firm was all about. Their openness to re-evaluating their own talent not only led to a breakthrough solution for the client and subsequent enthusiastic endorsement of the firm, but also led to the development of a new core competency. The firm is now positioned for more strategic consulting at the highest policy level.

In another example, an architect was leading a design team for an innovative new conference center for the disabled. When it was discovered that there was no computer workstation on the market that would allow the disabled user to operate it without assistance, the architect designed and oversaw the manufacture of a prototype with a variety of movable components. The delighted client authorized mass production of a previously nonexistent product. In today's practice, these are just a couple of examples of the many unique forms of value capture that firms have discovered.

Innovation happens in many ways, by ingenuity and openness to progress, by jumping outside the comfort zone and into the zone of experimentation. It often leads to new value and to revolutionary new success models.

We believe that in the future there will be even more blurring of those traditional boundaries in the professions. This will result in greater wealth, opportunity and satisfaction than at

any time in history for those who are ready to work with, rather
than against, the forces of change.

QUESTIONS

1. How will you redefine job descriptions in your firm?

2. How will you and your firm be more innovative?

3. What is your work for?

DESIGN MAKES THE DIFFERENCE

"The ultimate creation is the process of creativity itself."

THE DESIGN FUTURES COUNCIL

G ood design is not simply about excellence in the final building or product. It is a central part of the business process and how your organization is run. It is about how your projects are managed, how employees are hired and trained, and how the marketing process creates new clients and projects. The design of your organization—its processes and its quality of output—is what we call enterprise design.

The Design/Enterprise model is a crucial ingredient in competitiveness. Just as adding value is central to the design process, how an organization is being run is central to design. It is the blueprint of your organization and your life. You want to have fun, make money and expand your career in ways that are both meaningful to you and to your clients. You have talent, and you have made a significant investment in your future. You have been a part of some key initiatives that have established your career and your organization.

Don't lose sight of your goals. With the changes ahead, both expected and unexpected, how do you go forward to improve both your prosperity and your well being? Based on countless stories that have been told to us, you do so with active—not passive—initiatives that anticipate the new economy.

Here are some principles that have been collected from leaders of some of the most successful design firms around the world:

- Get on with the reinvention of your own sustainable future and be an entrepreneur of your life.
- Expect business down-cycles. See them as an opportunity. Look for new and infinite possibilities in a world of constant change—an economy where design will be even more important. By maintaining financial control you maintain creative control.
- Design your life and your firm's future, not just around meeting your client's current tangible needs, but on strengthening your enterprise.
- Organize each day around your priorities. Design your day and make it count.
- Build a community of trust in all of your relationships.
- Laugh—it's a barometer of a firm's health.
- Be known for your resilience and your ability to achieve results, even during times of uncertainty.
- Be an authority, but also be a role model of balance, judgment and constant learning.

Creating satisfaction is one of the key values for all in the design professions. It is, in reality, the people and not the firms who lead and improve the firm's competitiveness. Change management is a key core competency for leaders in this profession. In the future, design will be more important than ever before. Through design, better communities are created, the economy improves, and the quality of life is shaped. As a designer, you are in a unique position of influence with your clients, colleagues and family members. Be willing to change while you can. Leverage your design skills to make a difference—the value chain will not be complete without you.

QUESTIONS

1. What are your top three goals as a design professional?

2. What does good design mean to you?

3. How do you measure design leadership?

"We need a design that will thrust greatness upon our city...will a 6% fee work?"

FINANCES: GETTING YOUR REWARD

Doing work without getting paid is the surest road to failure. To create a vibrant and productive design enterprise, it's vital to realize that good financial management is just as important as design skill. Money is the fuel that enables you to practice design to the best of your ability, and profits are needed to finance growth—including new equipment, highly trained people, and better work space. For many architects and engineers, finance is often a foreign language, but this need not be the case. By understanding a few simple principles and applying them consistently, you'll be able to spend more productive time doing great design and eliminate worry about paying the rent. Remember that your clients are already fluent in the language of finance, so if you want to enhance their success, and yours as well, it pays to understand that money is a design tool.

THE PHILOSOPHY OF PROFIT

"When you see a good idea—search for a better one."

ROGER GODWIN

I n the design profession, complaints about compensation are common. Architects often compare their earning power unfavorably with doctors, lawyers and sometimes even plumbers. They resent that clients don't seem to recognize the value of what they do, or pay "fair" fees. Yet our research shows that by and large the client community has considerable respect for architects and values their professional advice. So why is it so hard for most firms to generate a decent bottom line?

There are several reasons. By far the most important is the attitude about profitability that pervades the profession, plus the fundamental misunderstanding about what profitability really means. Design is a curious blend of the creative and the technical. It is not always clear at the start of a project what the final result will be—that's part of the discovery and delight of design. Since the required level of effort is often somewhat fluid and can change significantly over the life of a project, fees based on a presumed cost structure for producing the work are almost always guaranteed to be wrong. As the project proceeds and becomes more complex, additional unanticipated effort, if uncompensated, inevitably erodes the bottom line.

Hence, thinking that profit is what's "left over at the end of a job" is a sure recipe for failure. Instead, think of profit as a cost of doing business, just like rent, salaries or other overhead. Build it into your management structure and your design process. Why? Because profit is an essential part of running a design firm; it is necessary to generate investment in growth, new staff, new technology, and a better workspace. A firm that is not making a healthy profit is only robbing itself of the ability to produce work to the best of its ability. Viewed this way, profit is actually one of your most important design tools. A chronic lack of profit is like a disease that attacks a firm's vital organs. You can't afford this, and neither can your clients.

Would you willingly patronize a doctor or a lawyer who had trouble paying bills and was on the verge of bankruptcy? No, and neither would your clients. Since many clients are business minded, they appreciate good business sense in others and understand that the fees they pay must cover the cost not only of the talent assigned to their job but the infrastructure of the firm as well. At the same time, clients are seeking value—they want real benefit for the fees that they are paying. Very often what happens is that the architect is tempted to perform services that are not needed or required by the client; the resulting cost only adds burden—not value—to the project.

What Is a Fair Return?

Most firms earn profits that are comparable to a standard certificate of deposit at your local bank. Why risk your time, capital, and professional liability on that basis, unless the practice of architecture is just a hobby? For firms that are willing to concentrate on adding value for their clients, profits in the 10

154   to 15 percent range and even higher are quite possible. Remember that the higher your legitimate profit, the better able you will be to serve your clients.

There are several ways to achieve better profit in your firm. Ironically, the most important aspect of profitability has nothing to do with money; it has to do with thoroughly understanding your clients' needs and constraints. At the onset of a new project or client relationship, ask:

• What does the client hope to achieve?
• What do they value?
• How can you help create that value?

When the answers to these questions are truly understood, you will have established the basis for an effective fee negotiation—one that benefits both sides. Don't concentrate on how much you are likely to make. That only clouds the issue from the client's perspective and your own. Instead, concentrate on how your firm is uniquely qualified to help your clients realize their goals. With this in mind, a reasonable fee—one that includes the opportunity for profit—is much easier to establish.

Good Design Creates Good Value

What about clients who have set predetermined fee limits or select design services primarily on the basis of low cost? When the fee limits are set before negotiation begins, as is often the case in government work, negotiate instead on the basis of scope or schedule. Provide what is reasonable for the fee available, and don't over-promise results.

Make sure you agree on what will trigger additional services, and then be vigilant about requesting them when circumstances warrant. Pressure on fees can actually be helpful because it forces firms to critically assess their production processes and weed out policies, procedures, and even staff that are not cost effective. Many companies have experienced the sweeping changes of re-engineering, which is a fundamental reconfiguration of how a business is organized and how it produces goods and services. Since the essential point is how to create value through productivity, why should the design professions be immune from this process?

In fact, you should welcome a serious discussion about value with any client, and then show how you are going to deliver the goods. Good design always creates good value. Be prepared to demonstrate how, and your negotiations will be much more satisfying.

Know What Kind of Work to Pursue

One of the most important ways to achieve profitability is through strategic marketing—knowing what kind of work to pursue and, equally important, what not to. If you understand the talent in your firm and how to make best use of it, you will be more focused in your marketing and better able to secure jobs for which you are truly qualified and therefore highly competitive.

Don't waste your time chasing projects with a low probability of success. And when you land a good one, negotiate intelligently making sure that there is a win/win outcome for all concerned. If you take on risk, insist on appropriate compensation. For example, when hiring consultants, don't forget to charge a premium to account for the management, communication, coordination, and liability associated with their work.

Don't accept uncompensated risk—it's a mistake for all concerned and sure to be a drain on profits.

Communicate Project Goals

When the job is landed and the contract terms are set, make sure that the entire design team understands the financial parameters of the job. People perform best when they are informed; they have to know what's important and how their activities make a difference not only to the design but also to the bottom line.

This is not to say that you should be running your design firm like a bank or an insurance company, but it does mean that good design and good management are complementary—one is not possible without the other. This is a fundamental principle. Bear in mind that project losses are extremely expensive. For example, if a project loses $100,000, it would take an entirely new $10 million job, at a 10 percent fee and a 10 percent profit, just to get back to break even. Losses on individual projects are not just an isolated, short-term problem—their effect is felt far into the future. Project losses are like a heavy tax.

The philosophy of profitability is relatively simple. Without profits, your ability to deliver top-quality design service is compromised, and the future of your firm is in jeopardy. While you may not be able to guarantee a profit on every single job, you can greatly increase your probability with a few simple steps: understand your clients' goals, find a way to demonstrate your value, negotiate accordingly, and then manage with vigilance.

And remember that "profit" is not a dirty word. Profitability is good for your firm and it is also good for your clients. A firm that is financially healthy is in a position to do a much better job. And after all, that's the bottom line.

QUESTIONS

1. Why are clients attracted to design firms that are run as good businesses?

2. What level of profit do you need to practice successfully?

3. How can you demonstrate to your clients that good design is good value?

PROFITABILITY BY DESIGN

"Identify the new rules—define your opportunity space—and position yourself for continuous improvement."

KERRY HARDING

For many design professionals, the financial aspects of the profession are viewed as a necessary evil, something that gets in the way of producing quality design. It is precisely because of this attitude that some design firms find themselves in chronic financial difficulty, unable to pay competitive salaries and bonuses, provide staff training, or acquire the most advanced technology to improve their productivity.

Surprisingly, this phenomenon is not so much related to skill as it is to attitude. It is time that designers, like their best clients, understand that profitability is an essential ingredient in a healthy practice and that good business management skills are not "anti-design" but in fact establish the very foundation that enables a firm to pursue and support its design mission.

Some architects still assume that profit is what's left over at the end of a job. Nothing could be further from the truth. Profitability, like good engineering, should be designed into a project at the start, and it begins with the basic assumption that design is a value-added enterprise.

Clients want top-quality design. They appreciate and are prepared to pay for professional services that will enable them to meet their goals. Like the rest of us, clients are subject to the market dynamics, and they are acutely aware of the cost/benefit ratio of their decisions. All of this should inform the design process and enable the architect to produce better results.

Understanding Risks and Rewards

Architects are often guilty of "creative interpretation" or willful misunderstanding of the client's specific goals for the project. When the task at hand is thoroughly understood by both stakeholders, creating a productive process for achieving those goals is greatly simplified.

Next time you are involved in a fee negotiation with a client, ask yourself the following simple questions:

- What does the client really need?
- What does the client value?
- How will the client measure the success of the project?
- How does the client measure cost, value and price?
- Is the architect selling what the client is buying?

For a fee negotiation to be successful there needs to be an exchange of value. The client must feel both understood and well served. This leads directly to setting fees that make sense for both sides—fees that include the opportunity for profit.

Profits Regenerate the Future

When negotiating with a client, remember that asking is the first rule in receiving. There must be enough of a fee on the table to produce the quality results that the client seeks. If both sides understand this, it will be a straightforward transaction. If the fee level is not sufficient to provide at least the opportunity for profit, then there is often a fundamental misunderstand-

160 ing of the scope of the engagement by either the owner or the architect. Why are profits important? Profits are important because they are necessary to support the design mission of the firm. Just breaking even is an inevitable ticket to oblivion.

REGENERATIVE FINANCIAL MODEL

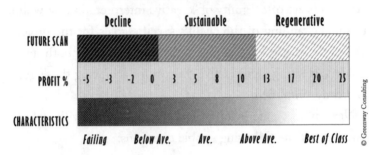

Make Growth an Objective

Any creative enterprise needs to grow in order to thrive. This growth can be measured in terms of dollars of revenue, numbers of people, or levels of talent and expertise. Growth requires fuel—for hiring and training talented staff, acquiring new technology and adapting to the inevitable changes in the marketplace. Growth is a risky business, often uncertain, yet it is growth that keeps an enterprise going.

Organizations that support growth on a personal and professional level are more likely to attract interesting commissions and talented people. As a result, these firms are better able to produce quality results than those that remain stagnant and hobbled by low profitability. In other words, profit should be seen as a cost of doing business, just like rent or salaries. Managing for profitability will enable a design firm to produce higher quality work, a greater level of client and staff satisfaction and a much more interesting future.

Market Strategically

How will this shift toward profitability take place? The first step is to market strategically: pursue only those commissions for which you can offer significant value added. Many firms waste precious marketing resources (time, money, and talent) chasing jobs for which they are only marginally qualified, resulting in frustration and an abysmal hit rate. By understanding the needs and desires of your prospective clients, you can focus your efforts on those prospects for which you can be realistically competitive. Being a true expert will not only improve your marketing results, it will give you a leg up in the negotiating process.

Negotiate Wisely

Intelligent negotiation is a crucial step in attaining profitability, and good listening is an important component in this. This requires both a thorough understanding of the commission as well as a thorough understanding of your costs. If the two don't balance, you are in trouble before you start. No amount of talent can rescue a bad contract.

Do not negotiate on the price of a job but on the value that will be delivered. This simple principle is often misunderstood. If you are not experienced in negotiation techniques, get help. Recognize that an unbalanced contract is bad for both parties. Also recognize that in addition to negotiating a fee, you can negotiate scope, time, deliverables, terms, and level of quality. If there is not a legitimate opportunity for profit in the contract, you will have created "voluntary misfortune" at the beginning of the job. The cost of an unprofitable project is enormous, not just in financial terms but in lost opportunity and staff morale. It is like borrowing from the future.

Establish a Simple Tracking System

Once you have negotiated the scope, schedule, and fee, it is extremely important to set up a simple but accurate tracking system that will enable you and your staff to understand the project's status at any time. These tracking systems must be objective and measurable—do not rely on subjective judgments or percentage completion estimates.

Many jobs run into trouble by failing to reserve predetermined portions of the fee for specific phases of the project. Hence the last phase, usually construction administration, is guaranteed to run a loss. When this happens it is too late to recover. This often leads to quality problems in the field, dissatisfied clients, and frustration all around. Apportioning the fee properly requires discipline and an understanding that all phases of the process are critically important to success. None can be compromised.

Non-Linear Solutions

The design process is creative, not linear. By definition, the answers are not clear at the beginning of a job—they have to be discovered during the course of design and given physical form. Because of this, changes in scope, schedule, and cost are not unusual. When this happens, it is time to revisit the terms of the contract and raise the issue of additional services with the client.

Many architects and designers will perform additional services as a gesture of goodwill without recognizing the true cost, which can include a substantial long-term liability. The recognition of risk and its associated rewards are always part of the profitability equation.

Designers are unique in their potential to deliver value to their clients. This value lasts far beyond the transaction for design services, often extending several generations into the future. For architects to deliver this value, they need healthy practices and this requires profitability. Planning for profit is no different in concept from planning for space or engineering requirements—it needs to be designed into the job at the outset as a clear expectation. Profit is not an accident; it is an essential ingredient of a high quality professional practice. It is part of what enables you to do you best for your clients.

QUESTIONS

1. Profitability starts with good listening. How do you know if you are a good listener?

2. What out-of-the-box idea will you implement to improve performance?

3. Is your financial model operating in the decline, sustainable, or regenerative zones? Why?

HOW TO RECOGNIZE THE VALUE YOU BRING TO CLIENTS

"You can't predict the future...but you can create it."

AROL WOLFORD

C hange is redefining professional practice. For example, some of you are taking the initiative to develop pre- and post-design services that expand both your revenue base and some very significant new profit centers. On the other hand, there are those who still say something like, "Well, I'm just an architect, and it's difficult to make money." Now, those aren't always the words that are used, but make no mistake, that is the message. The tone and the attitude form a subtle but convincing posture that leads nowhere. Do the clients see value? No, they see a negative and passive professional who is limiting the potential of the relationship before it even begins.

Economic indicators are changing for your clients—and they should be for you too. You can be more relevant than ever if you are creative and compassionate. While traditional practice can be respectable, there are many new opportunities that will take you far beyond traditional boundaries. Some firms are winning big, profitable new commissions and providing innovative new services, such as programming, site selection, financial model-

ing, facility management, annual building diagnostics, and productivity evaluations. These model firms are finding satisfying
challenges, good margins, and a high rate of repeat business.

Designers can advocate for creativity and innovation beyond
traditional problem solving. Architects don't just draft and draw;
engineers don't just calculate for structural strength; landscape
architects don't just select plant materials; and interior designers
don't just "decorate." Strange as it seems, these myths are still
present in many firms today. These stereotypes deflate the level
of respect and the perceived value of the professional services. We
believe good design can create added value for your clients in
many ways:

- Good design enhances communication.
- Good design improves safety.
- Good design saves time and money.
- Good design improves staff productivity.
- Good design simplifes use, manufacture, and performance.
- Good design enhances competitiveness and business success.
- Good design improves health and well being.
- Good design creates beauty and delight.

Successful firms stand apart from the pack. They are leaders—not followers—of creative design. Sometimes they break
the rules, and, thus, redefine the value propositions. Clients
notice and they spread the word. They understand that a value
driver is neither a firm's brochure nor a catch slogan—it is,
instead, a differentiating insight and an ability to put new ideas
into action.

QUESTIONS

1. What would you call yourself if you couldn't use your present professional title?

2. How creative is your culture? How do you know?

3. List the ways that you produce value for your clients.

"No project can be successful unless it is properly structured from the beginning, with clearly stated goals and identified challenges...the idea of starting a project off right is so critical and yet so often misunderstood."

M. ARTHUR GENSLER

Designers often complain about low fees and how difficult it is to be profitable when clients expect more service for less money. One of the obvious reasons for this is that clients are reluctant to spend when they don't understand what they are paying for.

Quality design embraces more than aesthetics—it also has a financial dimension. Does this mean that quality design is unimportant to clients or that they don't care what a project looks like? No, they care a great deal, which is why they hire architects and designers in the first place. However, they don't always understand how to value the design process or how to establish design fees. What are the benefits of good design? What are the true costs of poor quality design? How can the architect make a positive difference to the client's bottom line? These are the questions that architects need to articulate to their clients in order to rebalance the economic equation of risk and reward in professional practice.

When you start your next fee negotiation, try asking your client this question: "What are you trying to accomplish with this project and what is it worth to you to get it right?" Then use the discussion to understand what value the client is placing on design and how you can provide it. Portray your services in terms that the client can understand, using quantitative measures. Hourly rates are one way to do this, but they can be limiting and don't always reflect the fact that the value of good design continues long after the transaction is completed.

Sometimes the key value issue for a client is speed, such as being able to deliver a new academic building in time for the start of fall classes. Sometimes it is budget control—the ability to deliver at or below the prevailing cost for projects of a similar type. Sometimes it is design imagery—producing a memorable project that will attract tenants or that publicly symbolizes what is unique about the client's mission.

It helps to "unbundle" architectural services on a phase-by-phase basis and show the client the kinds of tasks that are necessary to get the desired results. It also helps to put specific limits on the number of hours, design options and the total length of the contract time that the fees will cover so that the client knows what he or she is getting for the money. One of the most important things to do in negotiation is to educate your client about how their internal decision-making processes affect the cost, speed, and quality of the entire project.

If you are experiencing difficulty in negotiating reasonable contracts, the chances are good that there is a communications glitch somewhere. The glitch can be external—coming to closure on just what the client has in mind and what it is worth; or it can be internal—getting your staff to understand how to deliver the goods within the parameters of the contract. Either way, it helps to demystify. Put yourself in your client's shoes—

what would inspire them to hire you? When you can answer
this question in terms that your *client* will understand, you're on
your way to a better structure.

QUESTIONS

1. Clients don't want to spend money on things they don't
   understand. How will you address this?

2. How can you use quantitative measures to explain the value
   of your services?

3. How will you make sure your clients are constantly informed
   about the value of a project?

REDESIGNING DESIGN FEES

"I found that money was like a sixth sense without which you could not make the most of the other five."

SOMERSET MAUGHAM

L et's look closer at fees by examining the frustrations of design professionals. Are you tired of skimpy design fees? Tired of consulting expenses that increase your liability while eating into your profits? Frustrated with clients who expect great service but can't seem to pay on time? If so, it's time to take charge of your finances. It's time to design a different way of doing business.

After all, if money matters frustrate you, the odds are that you're distracted from doing what you do best—creating great design solutions for your clients. It's time to stop complaining and get to work on the solution. First, realize that form, function and finance can all be viewed as design problems. And remember that it's in the client's best interest, as well as yours, to craft a financial relationship that makes sense—one that is easily administered and insures an exchange of value for both sides.

Value is a two-way street. Take a moment and ask yourself what the client is trying to achieve by hiring your firm. What are you providing? What are the special benefits that accrue because of your participation? How can the design solutions that you create bring extra value to the project? If you truly understand how this transaction looks from the other side of the table, you will then be in a position to approach negotiations with a win/win attitude rather than as a victim of circumstance.

If you cannot quantify design value for the client or distinguish your services from those of other firms, then, like it or not, you are in the commodities business. This means that you are a "price-taker"—subject to fee levels set by the marketplace, not determined by your special skills. This is not an inherently bad place to be if you realize that your primary value is offering low cost services. Your client will choose whichever firm can satisfy his or her needs at the minimum responsible fee. In this case, concentrate on reducing your cost of operations rather than negotiating higher fees because your value lies in creating efficiency.

On the other hand, if your firm has extraordinary design talent, special technical expertise or substantial experience in a certain building type, then you must learn how to translate that into bottom line results. Once again, learn to view this value from the other side of the table. Here are some suggestions:

1. **Always express value in terms that can be measured by the client.** Tell clients you can get the project done sooner, that you can design space that is measurably more efficient with a lower operational cost and that you can increase their staff productivity in specific ways.

2. **Put the right people on the job.** Utilize staff who truly understand the client's goals and whose skills are suited to creating the right solution. If such people do not exist in your firm, consider outsourcing portions of the assignment.

3. **Look for ways to simplify your accounting system.** Agree to bill for a set amount each month so that invoicing is

automatic and payments can be approved routinely. Send separate bills for fees and reimbursable expenses—don't let a dispute about a few dollars in travel charges hold up thousands of dollars in cash flow.

4. **Have a clear understanding about accounts receivable.** Know when to stop work or hold back on deliverables if payments are consistently late. If this sounds too harsh, then reverse the incentive and provide a discount to all clients who pay within ten days.

5. **Take pride in your business practices.** Make sure that they are best-of-class and that all of your staff understands how good management supports your mission to create good design.

6. **When busy, raise your prices.** When times are flush, you need to store up a few acorns for the inevitable lean times that come with every change in the business cycle.

7. **Always reserve a portion of your revenue for retained earnings.** Continually invest in the improvement of your firm and your people. Your staff is your human capital, and the smarter and better trained they are the more powerful your firm will be.

8. **Learn how to say "no thank you" to a commission if the fee is not sufficient for the job at hand.** If you take a loss on a project, it can prove to be extraordinarily expensive. Project losses are an unnecessary tax on your future.

The big lesson here is to run your firm with the same creative mindset that you apply to a design problem. What is the purpose of the organization? How does it function? How will it change over time? How can you creatively combine form, function and finance? Think of management not as a chore but as something that provides leadership to your people. Revenue is the lifeblood of any organization, so design your fees accordingly.

QUESTIONS

1. How will you create a financial relationship with your client that ensures an exchange of value?

2. How will you reduce your cost of operations without compromising quality?

3. How will you leverage your expertise or talents and translate that into bottom-line results?

CHARGING AHEAD—NEW FEE STRATEGIES

> "The will to win is important, but the will to prepare is vital."
>
> JOE PATERNO

O ne of the most common sticking points between clients and architects is the question of what constitutes a "fair" fee. Because design by its very nature is creative, its processes and outcomes are not always predictable. Yet clients, who often view the world with a management perspective, need to know what to expect. How much will the project cost? When will it be finished? What will I get for my money? These are questions that lurk in every negotiation, either above or below the surface. Surprisingly often, the architect's honest answer to these questions is, or should be, "I don't know."

Design is something of an exploratory adventure, and as the project proceeds there may well be changes to the program, budget, and schedule. These changes can be substantial. How is it possible to reconcile both the value and the uncertainty of design while still making good business sense for both sides?

First and foremost, it's important to recognize that every negotiation is fundamentally about an exchange of value. Each side gives something in order to get something. While it is tempting to think of this as a zero-sum game (I win/you lose), the unique quality of design is that it can create and not just transfer value. The difference is extremely important.

When you buy a product, the money you spend covers the basic cost of manufacturing and distribution plus an assumed profit margin. Cost of production is a primary price driver. However, in design, the cost of the "product" (drawings and models) often has little to do with the value of the service delivered. For example, when a client seeks advice about the development potential of certain commercial property, an architect may be able to render in only a few hours recommendations that are worth millions of dollars to the client. At the same time, it is possible for architects to spend days on details that have little or no intrinsic value from the client's perspective.

Setting design fees can be a confusing and frustrating exercise for everyone. Sometimes the legitimate needs of the client (speed or cost control, for example) may be interpreted by the architect as antithetical to good design. Sometimes the personal passion of the architect will get in the way of the client's goals.

Over many decades, a generally accepted linear process for most projects has come to be recognized by designers and clients alike. The sequence is simple and relatively clear, progressing from the general to the specific: schematic design, design development, construction documentation, and construction administration. This appetizer-main course-dessert mentality works to a point, but it ignores the strategic value that many architects are equipped to deliver but seldom able to articulate.

For instance, programming has traditionally been considered outside the scope of basic services, yet it is during this phase that the essence of a project's goals and values are defined, as well as its governing parameters of square footage and cost. A well-conceived program can save the client considerable time and money by making sure that the right project is being built in the first place. How much is such a program worth? About as much as a good map—the paper upon which it's printed is cheap, but its actual value is priceless if you happen to be lost.

The best way to approach fee negotiation is with the same attitude as a design problem itself—be creative when appropriate and definitive when necessary. Start by understanding from the client's perspective as much as you can about what it will take to make the project a success. Is it schedule, budget or function? The need to create an attention-getting building? Do not assume that your goals are the same as the client's. Only by seeing the design process through the client's eyes will you be able to communicate how to address those goals. For example, do you discuss food in terms of taste, appearance, nutrition, personal preference, cost, or aspects of all five? Only after you have a mutual understanding of what is at stake is it appropriate to discuss cost. Before you know what something should cost, you have to know its value. Value is the ratio of cost to benefit, and it is the fulcrum of compensation. Without a fulcrum there is no leverage either way.

There are many dimensions to a business deal and money is only one of them. Terms and conditions, time, limits of liability, publicity potential, the prospect of multiple projects with the same client and good references all play a role in negotiations. If you focus only on the money, you'll rob yourself (and your client) of the possibility of a fee structure with a custom fit.

In today's competitive environment, there are many factors in both getting a job and doing a job. Some clients come to the table with a predetermined notion of what to pay, and others **177**

really don't know what they want or how much it should cost.
Each and every situation will be different, and this is true even
when you do multiple projects for the same client or work for
government agencies that have established pricing policies
already in place.

Here are a few tips to demystify your fee strategy:

- **Do your homework.** Find out as much as you can about
  similar projects, their costs, and fees. This will help establish an objective point of reference for both sides.

- **Break the big job into smaller units and negotiate each one
  separately.** This is especially useful in projects that might
  have to undergo a complex public approvals process or for
  projects that are likely to last several years.

- **Negotiate for your consultants separately.** This will give
  you the opportunity to apply a mark-up on their services to
  cover your management time and the professional liability
  that you bear for their work.

- **Distinguish between fee for service and reimbursable
  expenses.** Reimbursable expenses have low intrinsic value to
  the client. Whenever possible, charge a reasonable mark-up
  to cover the cost of your cash flow.

- **When you cannot reliably predict how much a project will
  cost, charge by the hour until both you and the client have
  a better handle on things.** Hourly rates encourage both
  sides to be productive and efficient, and they take away
  uncertainty. You can convert to a fixed fee or a percentage
  fee whenever it is mutually agreeable.

- **Consider other forms of "currency" as a basis for compensation.** Stock warrants, stock options and fees based on the

client's increase in profits or revenue flow as a result of the project are all options. This ties your financial destiny to the success of the project and realigns incentive. By being creative and redefining the risk/reward equation, some firms are producing dramatic increases in revenues and profits.

A good business relationship between you and your client is essential to good design. It will focus your creativity and will make billing and collections much easier and more predictable, increasing your cash flow. It will enable you to put your energy into what matters most—producing results for your clients. If you approach the fee strategy question with a similar mindset, you can turn your client's attention from the question of, "What is this costing me?" to "How can I get the best value?" When both the client and the architect are thinking in terms of value rather than cost, the discomfort in setting fees will start to evaporate.

QUESTIONS

1. How will you learn to negotiate better?

2. What are your new fee strategies?

3. How can your firm provide new, profitable services?

> "...a traditional bureaucratic structure, with its need for predictability, linear logic, conformance to accepted norms, and the dictates of the most recent 'long range' statement, is a nearly perfect idea killing machine."
>
> JERRY HIRSHBERG

All firms have the ability to control their costs better. Yet year after year design firms insist on putting line items into their budgets for things that actually can cause a firm to fail rather than succeed. We call these budgeted but non-strategic expenses failure costs. Look around at your own operation. You no doubt will find failure costs imbedded in your system; they are in fact quite common.

To be most effective, you want to align your talent and resources to deliver results to your clients in the most cost effective way. The right steps will improve business and organization performance. Yet in many firms, profit and high performance are not values held by all managers. Some are motivated by something other than the financial health of their organizations. For instance, they want their firm to grow regardless of costs, or to enter expensive design competitions, or to achieve harmonious employee relations and high morale at any cost, or they want the opportunity to belong to a golf club or to travel to interesting and expensive places at company expense.

Insuring the financial health of an organization must become a priority of the leaders in the firm. Successful firms make it a hallmark of their culture. Lean management can be satisfying—not just smart business. Controlling costs means improved profitability. It's worth getting passionate about.

Tips for Driving Out Failure Costs:

1. Cut your supply budgets. Every cost should be evaluated based on how it supports productivity.

2. Analyze technology costs. After conducting technology audits in firms we have found that most firms are wasting money on both hardware and software. In certain instances they get software updates that are not needed and are never used. Yet because these are budgeted for, they get purchased and then wasted.

3. Travel expenses can often be reduced without harming the relationships with clients. Look for reductions of 10 to 15 percent.

4. Telephone hardware and long distance service offer many new savings. With pace of change in the telecommunications industry we find that it is wise to check often to make sure that you are using the lowest-cost long distance carrier. Cell phone costs are being dramatically reduced. Several firms have achieved cost savings of 5 to 15 percent a year for the last two years.

5. Office space is often a way to reduce fixed overhead. Go for functional, creative spaces, not for the spacious and luxurious. One firm reported moving to a tall-ceilinged warehouse space. This reduced their rent by 45 percent, and they gained a more creative work atmosphere in the bargain.

6. Many failure costs are found in the human resource budgets. We're not just talking about marginal performers and the dead wood that should be cut, but also making smart decisions such as the introduction of a flexible benefits program. Consider a pay effectiveness audit, a staffing analysis, a turnover-costing model geared for new optimization, and a comprehensive review of benefits.

7. When cost control needs to be dramatic because of severe economic difficulty, look at short-term incentive compensation tied to measurable improvements in efficiency. You may also want to reduce or freeze bonuses and even base pay if the situation warrants.

8. Benchmark your health plan's performance to determine if your benefits package is competitive.

9. Review current pricing agreements with vendors. Ask for discounts. You may also wish to conduct a claims audit to determine vendor inefficiencies and identify weaknesses.

10. Ask your recruiting agencies for ways to bring down costs. You may find a willingness to renegotiate agreements.

11. Leverage the use of the Internet as a recruiting and communications tool.

12. Control mailing and shipping costs. Be certain that overnight delivery costs are reimbursable.

13. Rethink your marketing costs. Cutting costs, even drastically, may not impair hit rate performance.

14. Mentor and coach your staff on performance and profitability issues. Others in the firm will be watching you—not so much what you say as what you do to show your commitment to a lean, high performance organization.

"Everyone agreed the old way
of budgeting took too long."

Design organizations need to control costs in both good times and bad. Keep these priorities in mind:

- **1990's Focus:** Growing the firm and hiring more staff.
- **Today's Focus:** Cost control and cutting expenses such as operational and staffing costs.
- **Tomorrow's Design/Enterprise Focus:** Lean culture that keeps clients satisfied and retains top talent.

Design professionals should not only care about design excellence and good service with respectable profits, they should also have an absolute commitment to lead their organizations in a way that eliminates failure costs from their culture.

1. What are the "failure costs" imbedded in your current budgets?

2. How will you streamline your operations?

3. How and when should you consider downsizing to stay fit and healthy in an economic downturn?

MARKETING

❑ **Avoid expensive design competitions.** Design competitions are like dating bars—the attraction is based on first impressions only. Design competitions don't give you—or the client—the opportunity to think deeply about a project and give it the effort that it deserves. They are also extremely expensive. Entering a competition can easily cost $25,000 and more, and this is equivalent to getting a new $5 million project at a 5 percent fee and making a 10 percent profit. Instead, invest that same $25,000 to improve your marketing in other ways.

❑ **Calculate your cost of sales.** "Cost of sales" is the amount of time and money it takes to land $1 in new fees. Make sure that your cost of sales is less than your profit margins. If you spend 10 percent of your revenue on marketing but are only making 8 percent profits, you are slowly but surely going out of business. Evaluate your entire marketing program with cost of sales in mind.

❑ **Don't market by mail.** Responding to RFPs or public lists of projects without prior personal knowledge of the job is a very low probability way to get work. Get to know the decision-makers in advance (even those in large government agencies). If you don't know the key people on the client side, look for other opportunities.

❑ **Nurture repeat work.** Repeat business is by far and away the least expensive marketing you can do. Look for clients who are likely to have ongoing needs, and find a way to stay on their radar screen. Taking lots of smaller projects will provide face time (and profits) and position you for the larger projects when they come up.

❑ **Promote personal contact.** Clients hire people, not brochures. Personal contact is the basis of trust. Lunches, dinners, museum outings, sporting events, or an evening at the theater are great ways to get to know clients as people. Become active in local boards or your clients' professional organizations as well.

❑ **Professional organizations.** Active involvement in professional organizations is a great way to extend your network, learn new ideas, and build relationships. Don't just be a member—be a leader. Get on steering committees, nominating committees, and boards. Organize national meetings and preside at seminars. Visibility translates easily into credibility.

❑ **Provide innovative services.** Help your clients obtain financing. Navigate them through the approvals process at city hall. Create alliances with other professional consultants, providing an expanded menu of services. Find out where the gaps are and fill them. You'll be surprised how this will expand your marketing horizons.

❑ **Unbundle your services.** Rather than negotiate long-term contracts, consider subdividing your services into smaller, bite-sized pieces. This makes it less risky for the client to try you out, and easier to focus on doing a good job for a specific task. Try charging fixed rate prices for specific services, such as programming. Develop new rate structures (cost per square foot, cost per sheet of drawings, fixed average hourly rate for all office staff, etc.) that will make it easier and more predictable for your clients to use your services.

OPERATIONS

❑ **Budget, budget, budget.** Finding out how much profit you have left at the end of a job is like driving down the street using only your rear-view mirror. Instead, establish key parameters of time and money before you begin, and then use them to guide your progress. Budgets are like guardrails— they are intended to keep you on the road. Use them.

❑ **Keep your project team intact.** Changing personnel mid-stream almost always throws a project off balance. Instead, get the right team in place in the beginning and then leave it alone until the job is done. This builds commitment on both sides of the street, and makes for better results all around. It's also a great way to teach younger staff about the integrated process of design.

❑ **Use state-of-the-art technology.** Keep your software and your licenses current. Get the best equipment you can afford, and leverage its use on every project. Remember that machines are always less expensive than people, so maximize your staff efficiency by giving them the best tools.

❑ **Outsource.** Many services provided in-house can be outsourced. Printing, model-making, specification writing, and even project accounting are a few examples. Keep your staff lean and totally focused on the job at hand, and hire out the rest. This can reduce management headaches and help you turn on a dime when necessary.

TIPS FOR ACHIEVING SATISFYING PROFITS

❏ **Encourage personal responsibility.** Establish accountability at all levels of your organization and enforce it. Promote those who do well and reassign under-performers, especially at the senior levels of the firm. Do not tolerate a laissez-faire attitude.

❏ **Attack problems early.** If you wait until the end of a job to confront problems, they will never get solved. Train your staff to get you the bad news as soon as possible when you still have time to do something about it. This is the only way to turn bad news into good news.

❏ **Read the contract.** Encourage every key member of the project team to read the contract. In fact, insist on it. Knowing the extent of your responsibilities—and the client's—is the best way to make sure that mutual expectations are met. Understanding the contract terms will trigger much better performance at all levels of the project team.

❏ **Be alert to additional services.** All projects have some element of risk and the unknown. When conditions change, discuss the implications with your client. Changes can affect schedule, budget, scope of work, and design quality. When discussing additional services, always focus on the value to the client, not your own pocket.

PROFESSIONAL SERVICES

❏ **Link profitability and design value.** Make the relationship between good design and good business practice one of your firm's core values. Good design is good business, and good business practice is good for design. If you can't demonstrate this argument, who will?

❏ **Get out of the vendor trap.** Do your clients see you as only a low-cost producer of commodity services? If so, change your strategy and find a way to provide unique value, something that no one else can do as well as you can. Then, even in a competitive market, you will have no competition.

❏ **Hire the best talent.** This is true up and down the line. Get the best design and technical staff, and also the best secretaries, accountants, and support staff. Hire the best consulting engineers, and seek work with the best contractors. In the long run, quality is always faster and cheaper, the networking is a lot better.

❏ **Delegate responsibility and authority.** Now that you've hired the best people, use them to their fullest. Don't try to be a hero and do everything yourself. The more you rely on your staff, the more they will be able to do for you, and the more you can do for them. Everybody wins.

❏ **Use profits to promote design quality.** Don't just talk about making more money—use it to improve everything you do. Get better space, buy better equipment, hire better people, do better photography of your projects, and so forth. When people understand that profitability makes a difference in design quality, they will perform even better.

❏ **Deliver what you promise on time.** This promotes better time management, improves efficiency, and builds credibility all around. If you finish on time, you'll make better decisions and your profitability is almost assured.

TIPS FOR ACHIEVING SATISFYING PROFITS

FINANCE

❑ **Tax yourself.** Try banking 10 percent of every incoming check—without exception—in a special untouchable profit account. Even if everything else runs at a break even, this insures a decent year-end result.

❑ **Mark up your consultants.** You are legally and professionally liable for the work that your consultants do on a job. Cover this risk by charging 10 percent to manage, coordinate, and deliver their work as part of your services. Alternatively, delete them entirely from your billing and have owners contract with them directly (they'll soon see the wisdom of the 10 percent markup).

❑ **Charge "plumber's rates."** If you don't know what a job is likely to cost, don't guess. Instead, use standard hourly rates until the scope of work and schedule are clarified. When in doubt, use "plumber's rates"—they compare favorably with those used by most architects!

❑ **Collect your bills.** Every month, review your accounts receivable and call the clients who have not paid. If there is a problem, work it out. Unlike wine and cheese, old bills do not improve with age.

❑ **Link performance and compensation.** Everybody in a firm knows who the non-performers are. Looking the other way doesn't help. Reassign them, retrain them, or help them find a new job, but don't let them fester in unproductive roles. Value your top performers with salaries, bonuses, and raises to build a productive culture.

❑ **Never shrink from additional services.** Most projects will produce about 10 percent in legitimate additional services, more than most average firm profit margins. If you ignore them, you are tacitly deciding to run a break-even operation. Good clients will pay for the additional value they receive, but you have to ask first.

❏ **Create innovative fee structures.** Stock options, stock warrants, bonuses based on schedule and budget control, or fees based on ongoing maintenance services are a few of the ways innovative firms are restructuring their fees. There is pressure on fees across the board, even in busy times, so get creative.

❏ **Demystify your accounting.** If your project staff doesn't understand your accounting system, it's not doing you much good. Discard the arcane and confusing spreadsheets and figure out how to explain the essentials on one piece of paper. Financial reports should be accessible to everyone whose performance will be influenced by them.

❏ **Automate time cards and billing systems.** Computers can track most everything quickly, easily, and accurately. Set up your timecards and billing systems to be automatic, and make sure that everyone, principals included, comply. If you can't track it, you can't bill it or manage it.

❏ **Use computer tracking.** For express mail, copying logs, overnight shipping, inventory supply, fax logs, and so forth, automate all your tracking systems and integrate with billing. Charge a 10 percent premium above cost and capture that lost revenue.

❏ **Negotiate long-term discounts.** Do you have favorite engineers? Would they be willing to cut their fees 5 percent in return for a guaranteed amount of work each year? Do you buy all your paper from one source? Would they be willing to give you a discount in return for guaranteed business? Leverage your volume, save money, and improve service all at the same time.

LOSE YOUR LOSERS

"We find ourselves in unprecedented circumstances—we need to rethink everything."

HON. RICHARD SWETT

I n the design business, it is taken for granted that some projects make money and others are destined to be losers. This assumption is so ingrained in the design professions that it's hardly given a second thought. In fact, working on a money-losing project is sometimes seen as a badge of honor—people can easily delude themselves into thinking that practicing until the money is all gone somehow makes for better design.

Great design comes from doing things right in the first place, not from making repeated mistakes. Nonetheless, many designers still labor under a fundamental misconception about the relationship between design quality and profitability. Far from being mutually exclusive, the truth is that they are mutually dependent—you can't have one without the other.

It's common wisdom that it isn't what you make, it's what you keep that counts. Accordingly, one of the best ways to protect profitability is by examining your losers. What went wrong? Why? Who was responsible? This is important because losers are double negatives—they not only rob the firm of today's profits, they place an invisible mortgage on your future operations as well.

There are several reasons that jobs end up in trouble. The first and most obvious is that the contract was not properly negotiated. Either you underestimated the amount of effort it would take to produce the job, or your project leadership permitted the team to get off track. Both of these conditions are fixable. Negotiation techniques can be learned, and if you have chronic problems in this area, don't be too proud to get expert training; it will pay you back many times over.

If you have difficulty predicting a project's cost over several years' duration, try breaking the contract into smaller pieces and agree to set fees sequentially one phase at a time. This will give both you and your client a much better way to establish value for your services as things develop, eliminating the guesswork for both sides.

De·sign·a·saur, *n*

As for project leadership, it's very important to provide clear and realistic expectations about profitability at the outset of each job. Make sure that appropriate staff is available, and establish true accountability for results. Without accountability, profit goals are meaningless.

At the end of each fiscal year, you can evaluate the effectiveness of your project managers by tallying up how many projects of what size were produced, how many fee dollars were managed, what the average utilization rate was and how many dollars of profit were generated. These measures are simple to produce and very telling. Don't try to manage your design firm without them.

If you have a problem project, sometimes the best you can hope for is to break even, but breaking even trumps a loss every time. Review the contract thoroughly to make sure that the entire team, including your consultants, understands the project requirements and also to make sure that you are charging for all legitimate additional services. Determine the minimum effort that will be required to get the job done with quality results, and don't accept the common complaint that it can't be done. There is always a better, cheaper, faster and more creative way to work, and often these solutions only reveal themselves under pressure. Whatever it takes, stop the bleeding at once and don't let it recur.

Another common source of project losses is accounts receivable. If you have trouble collecting your fees, call your clients directly and find out why. Sometimes the problem is a glitch in the accounting system; your billing protocols and those of your client don't match. This is not a surprise since many clients have unique payment policies. Learn what they are for each and

Bill separately for fees and expenses. Don't let a dispute about a $10 phone bill hold up payment of thousands of dollars in legitimate fees. If your clients are chronically late in their payments, tack on the interest and insist that it be paid. If portions of your bills are in dispute, get paid for the part that's not and resolve the rest as soon as possible. It's best for both you and your client that any misunderstandings are cleared up immediately and not allowed to recur. If your clients still don't pay on time, fire them. Instead of working for them at a loss, find other clients who value what you can do for them and are willing to pay fees that make economic sense.

Design competitions are another common source of losses that can be easily avoided. Except in extraordinary circumstances, where a reasonable stipend is provided or you have special knowledge or expertise about the project, competitions are a high-risk, low probability way to get work. They are also one of the worst possible ways for a client to choose an architect, since selection is based primarily on first impressions. There is no time to develop a deeper understanding of the client's site, budget and program. If you get the urge to enter a competition, even for a commission that you would dearly like to win, resist the temptation. Rather than roll the dice, use those same marketing dollars and the creative energy of your staff in much more productive ways.

Once you have cleaned up your losers, concentrate on changing your corporate culture about profitability. Make sure that your staff understands why profits are important and how they will be used to improve the firm. Insist on timesheet compliance by all, especially senior staff (weekly is minimum, daily is better). Conduct regular reviews by your project managers, identifying impending problems before they spin out of control. Address them right away and you will eliminate project losses; allow them to go untended, and they will grow exponentially.

Take the mystery out of profitability by training your staff about budgeting, staffing and delivering the goods on time and within budget. Make it clear that profitability is an integral part of the design mission of your firm, reinforcing the belief that "losses are for losers." You will find that you attract better staff and better clients in the bargain. Why? Because fundamentally, profits are a measure of value. And if you can't create value, both for your clients and your staff, you're in the wrong business.

QUESTIONS

1. If you had to fire a client, who would it be? Why?

2. How can your contracts and documents serve your quality and profit goals?

3. What are the productivity speed bumps in your organization?

As some of you have guessed, today's
agenda is green and sustainable design

THE ANATOMY OF LEADERSHIP

Effective marketing, efficient operations, creative design, and prudent financial management are all essential ingredients for success. What's needed most, however, is leadership. You need to communicate your passion for excellence for your clients and your staff, provide the means and methods to make it happen, and inspire others to commit their time and talent to the greater good. Good leaders are "downfield blockers"—they clear a path so that others can do their best work. And don't forget that good leadership goes beyond the walls of your firm to touch the community at large. Good design is a value-added enterprise—it always produces benefit in excess of cost—and it depends upon leadership to make it happen. Remember that ultimately, you're in the leadership business and design is your medium.

ARE YOU SURE YOU WANT TO CHANGE?

"The trouble with the future is that it usually arrives before we're ready for it."

ARNOLD GLASOW

H ere is a familiar problem. A firm principal says that he wants to change but then proceeds to spend most of his time resisting it. Growth has slowed, and so has the excitement. This design principal has become more complacent and less of a leader. A lot of time is spent living in the past. Once hot, the firm is now having trouble shifting gears to keep up with other firms that once trailed them. Quietly, inside the firm, the employees are hoping that something or someone will influence this principal to wake up and change his ways. Yet, he stubbornly resists change.

Here are some of the signs of firm stagnation:

1. Creating ideas is easier than implementing them.
2. Talk of change takes place—yet the same behavior and habit patterns persist.
3. Intellectual conversation takes place, but there is little follow-up action.
4. Adoption of the latest technology tools is lagging other firms.
5. The work hours are still long, but the outputs are noticeably less exciting.

6. Harsh judgments are made of others in the firm.

7. There is little mentorship and too much intimidation.

You don't have to go stale as you age. This century has been filled with architects and designers who have had their brightest moments in their later years. Remember the work of Buckminster Fuller, Congressman and ardent supporter of the arts Sidney Yates, architectural patron Jonas Salk, M.D., and hundreds of others. Their life work was only just beginning at age seventy. The challenge to stay current is not easy at any age, but by setting goals and through self-discipline, the objective can be met.

Each of us needs someone to deal with us honestly and openly about our shortcomings. It is our professional responsibility to dig deep inside ourselves and open ourselves to change. We can learn to be elastic, open to new methods and new behavior patterns. When we open ourselves to change, we grow and we help others around us grow as well. True professionalism must include an openness to change—and new pathways to success.

QUESTIONS

1. What are signs that your firm is becoming less relevant?

2. What fears are keeping you from achieving your dreams?

3. What changes are you willing to make in order to achieve greater success?

FASTER, SMARTER, BETTER—NEW DYNAMIC RULES

"Charge by your worth, not by the hour."

RAYMOND F. MESSER

I t seems that a lot of us are experiencing longer days and working in high stress environments. Most agree that the world of design is moving at a fast clip. Faster is not necessarily smarter. What are the implications for firm principals who want to keep their firms competitive?

Leading change is an ongoing challenge. Firm principals who are unprepared for change management often view change as the enemy. Whether you are prepared or not, you are functioning in an environment that includes taking risks and making choices. Bad choices can bring down the firm. A basic precept in management is, "where there is choice, there is change."

Where does this put you? Are you leading change with entrepreneurial zeal or are you in the "ready, fire, aim" category, overwhelmed by the day-to-day pressures? There is a better way. In fact, some firms are changing their "corporate DNA" in ways that are positive, productive and profitable.

Some firms are generating new services and capturing more of the client's attention and money. They understand that the profession of architecture and design may be mature in certain ways, but that the business of architecture is in its adolescence.

Yes, even in recessions, design and architecture can be a growth business.

Here's a checklist for becoming faster, smarter, better.

1. **Stop going to the same meetings and conferences.** Break away from habit patterns that are holding you back. Force yourself to spend more time with your clients and get closer to their major issues and concerns. Attend strategic conferences that help you visualize new and relevant pathways toward growth.

2. **Articulate your vision—often.** Work on putting that vision statement into day-to-day language so that the people around you can believe it. Reclarify your values and energetically live your values.

3. **Be more forceful in the way you communicate the urgency of change.** There are reasons for immediate change, so express them. Mobilize around those reasons. As you steer change, don't get discouraged—dig deeper for the energy to lead.

4. **Take a resilient attitude toward change.** Overcome the usual resistance and inertia. Remind those who doubt you that it's important to look from the outside in.

5. **Redesign your organization.** If you are to become faster, smarter and better, the balance of power in the firm will have to shift. Change and power are often at odds. Be up front and willing to face these issues.

6. **Benchmark and deliver.** Monitor and measure everything in your organization that you can. Even with a good strategy in place, if there is no accountability, action will be too slow to achieve your desired results.

7. **Actively communicate.** Take steps to meet more often

with your staff, but for shorter periods of time. Send an action summary around the office highlighting the positive results and benefits of your redesign. Use humor to reassure and motivate.

Change management is a key skill for twenty-first century managers. You have no doubt heard the saying, "I'm so busy with emergencies, I don't have time to do what's important." Change can be dangerous, yet the need to change is undeniable. Wise change creates design organizations that are retuned to be faster, smarter and better. Remember that competitive advantage is temporary—so think deeply, not just quickly.

QUESTIONS

1. How are you leading change in your organization?

2. How are you communicating urgency?

3. What key benchmarks do you use to measure your organization's productivity?

STABILITY = CHANGE

"Don't be cool. Cool is conservative fear
dressed in black. Free yourself from limits of
this sort."

BRUCE MAU

A rchitecture is a curious profession. Its products
(buildings) are static, but its process (design) is anything but. While it is true that buildings are made of
"sticks and stones" (and glass and steel and concrete), they are
also made of a host of intangibles—ambition, desire, conflict
and politics, to name a few. These intangibles are like a gas that
permeates the design process. Its presence is perceived but
rarely understood.

Architects are constantly called upon to reconcile seemingly
contradictory things—the ambitions of the clients vs. their limited resources; the scope of the program vs. the constraints of
the site; the need to meet a deadline vs. the desire to do it right.

Eventually, the intangibles congeal, a design emerges, and the
desire and ambition begin to condense into physical form,
which eventually becomes a building. There are many ways to
characterize this process, but it is often very hard for architects
to articulate it in terms that their clients or the public truly
understand. This is probably why it is so hard to negotiate fees
based on value rather than cost.

Each and every design project is unique—different client, different site, different budget, different program, different sched-

ule, different design goals and a different team. Even people who work together constantly change as they gain experience.

As a result, it should come as no surprise that there is an almost desperate desire to find any system, protocol, policy or procedure by which the design process can be codified and made more predictable and manageable. We not only have to fight the battle of communication and persuasion with our clients; we have to do the same with our colleagues, consultants and contractors on a constant basis.

As a way of dealing with this organized chaos, firms often adopt policies and procedures that are intended to create some measure of stability. If only we could do things in a standardized way on a consistent basis, they think, results might improve. There would be a higher level of quality, more predictability, greater speed and improved profit margins.

Thus, we make charts and graphs and schedules and budgets and diagrams, and we hold retreats and concoct strategic plans—all for the purpose of creating some measure of organization in our professional practices. This is understandable but too often fruitless. The marvel is that we keep doing it without getting the results that we are looking for.

"Stability" is not stable. The reason is simple, but hard to grasp. "Stability" is a process, not a state of being. "Stability" is actually a coping mechanism, an approximation rather than a destination. Dr. Sherwin Nuland, Yale physician and author, describes it this way in his book *The Wisdom of the Body*: "A stable system is not a system that never changes. It is a system that constantly and instantly adjusts and readjusts in order to maintain such a state of being that all necessary functions are permitted to operate at maximal efficiency. Stability demands change to compensate for changing circumstances. Ultimately, then, stability depends on instability."

This simple description shows how a common phenomenon can be commonly misunderstood. To get "stability," we have to constantly adjust everything that we do. Like the rider on a bicycle, we can only keep our balance by constantly moving forward. If we stand still, we fall over.

Successful firms are always monitoring their environment for signs of change and then adjusting accordingly. Status quo is not good enough, even if the status quo is good. What does this mean for your practice?

- Do you know what your clients are up to and what their needs will be next year?
- If you are unsuccessful at going after a project, do you take the time to find out why and then change your marketing approach?
- Do you constantly search for new management aids, such as financial software, that will enable your project teams to be better informed about where things stand?
- When you have trouble collecting timesheets from your staff or bills from your clients, do you do something about it?

In recent years many enterprises, both large and small, have learned the lesson about change and stability, sometimes the hard way. There is scarcely a market, product, service or an industry that has not been re-engineered, downsized, reinvented or made extinct in recent years.

Because it challenges our familiar concept of what is right or good, change can cause a great deal of stress. But it is also exhilarating because it extends our capacity to be productive. Firms that cling to fond memories of their past successes and wish to emulate them as they "reinvent their future" are in trouble. Those who cherish those memories for what they are and look for ways to use them as a springboard for continual improvement are much better positioned for success, even as they encounter the inevitable bumps in the road.

This is where the search for stability comes in. Stability does not come from not changing, it comes from continual reassessment and a willingness to retain what works and discard what doesn't. Perhaps this explains why even in the best and busiest of times, those in a position of leadership do not allow themselves to become complacent. The smartest among them always feel a little unsure and uncertain about the future. In their search for stability, they are always a bit on edge. If you seek stability in your firm, you have to stay in motion, stay alert and stay nimble. Standing still is just another way of falling behind.

QUESTIONS

1. Are you willing to change? How do you know?

2. Are you asking stupid questions? Smart people do it all the time.

3. Are you taking enough risks?

FOUR PARADOXES IN
DESIGN LEADERSHIP

"Control your destiny...or someone else will."

NOEL TICHY

Historians like to remind us that the only constant in life is change. Change is both wonderful and worrysome. In only a few short years, we have seen the birth of the information age, the collapse of the Soviet Union and a World Cup for U.S. women's soccer. What has gone up has come down. What once seemed impossible is now old hat. And what did not exist only a few years ago is now reshaping how we do business. Think back just two decades ago, before the advent of e-mail, voice mail, cellular phones, faxes, desktop publishing, word processing, Federal Express or the Internet. Indeed, it seems that change and contradiction have become our context.

Change is a scary thing, but it is necessary, and it is also unavoidable. Without change, there is no growth. With change comes uncertainty, but it also brings possibility. The irony is that while architects and designers are literally in the business of making physical changes in the lives of their clients, they are for the most part reluctant to embrace change in their own professional practices. For example, design is one of the last major industries to understand the value of marketing and branding, and one of the last to embrace computer technology.

It's time to get with the program. It's time to understand that contradiction is not an enemy. On the contrary, it is the land "between opposites" where real creativity lies. Here are some of the contradictions that drive the design professions today:

1. **Charge less but make more.** Let's face it, the world is a competitive place, and that's not altogether bad news. Competition breeds new ideas and innovation. These days, there is more pressure than ever on fees. Charge less, but make more by being innovative. Broadband your services, trade for equity rather than cash, reinvent your delivery systems for "warp speed." If you don't do this, someone else will.

2. **Work faster but do a better job.** There are countless examples from other industries of how to do more with less. Microwave meals, ATMs and on-line stock trading are only a few. Why should design be immune? Instead of complaining, become an innovator and lead the way.

3. **Be high tech but also high touch.** Put off by technology? Can't program that VCR? Get over it. Technology is a servant, not a master. Rather than drown in data, figure out a way to humanize it. Keep your life simple and focused, starting with memos limited to one page only. Use technology to communicate, not confuse. Invest in the best technology available. If you can't master it, hire somebody who can drive technology for you.

4. **Get better design by doing better business.** Good design and good business need not be natural enemies. In fact, they are closely aligned: You can't have one without the other. It's time to understand that creativity, innovation and results are good business values as well as good design

values. It's also time to understand that only profitable design firms will be able to invest in the technology, space and talented staff that will keep them viable tomorrow. Want to be a better designer? Run a better business. And vice versa.

Designers are able to bring uncommon value to their clients. They are able to visualize problems and devise solutions that work in three-dimensions. They understand the fundamental relationships among form, function and finance. They know the power of aesthetics. The very best are not bound by convention—they think outside the box. In today's changing world, these are leadership skills as well as design skills.

QUESTIONS

1. How are you listening carefully for changes and trends?

2. How will your firm address the paradoxes in design leadership?

3. How is your firm positioned for new levels of success?

SOLVING THE RIGHT PROBLEMS

"Markets can remain irrational longer than
you can remain solvent."

JOHN MAYNARD KEYES

The need for smart thinking and assertive problem solving has never been greater. Yet, many in the design professions suffer from myopic problem-solving capabilities. This is serious because their future is at stake.

Talking is one thing, and most in the design professions can talk problem solving with great aplomb. Those who get results are in quite another league. The league of innovators and the success-oriented are those who will not become "designasaurs." Those who are effective problem solvers know how to cut through complex issues, ask the right questions and solve the right problems.

One of the resources that we have been using to address this issue is a book by Ian Mitroff, a distinguished professor at the University of Southern California's Business School, called *Smart Thinking for Crazy Times: The Art of Solving the Right Problems*. Mitroff offers five key problem areas:

1. **Picking the wrong stakeholders:** It's almost always a bad idea to involve only a small set of stakeholders in formulating a problem.
2. **Selecting too narrow a set of options:** It is vital to produce

at least two different formulations of any problem.

3. **Framing a problem incorrectly:** By using a narrow set of disciplines, design functions, or variables, you often address only the symptoms, not the real problem.

4. **Setting the boundaries of a problem too narrowly:** Broaden the scope of every important problem just beyond your comfort zone.

5. **Failing to think systemically:** It's all too easy to focus on a part of the problem instead of the whole, to focus on the wrong part of a problem, and/or to ignore connections.

Understanding your ability to do this is your value as a leader in your organization—a value all too uncommon.

QUESTIONS

1. Take three clients and imagine how they feel about you and your organization. How would they describe your firm behind your back?

2. Look at your agenda for the next week. How can your firm turn the five key problems into advantages?

WHY BANKS ARE NO LONGER BUILDINGS

"It isn't that they can't see the solution. It is that they can't see the problem."

G.K. CHESTERTON

Once upon a time, banks and churches were the two most prominent structures in town. Banks symbolized reliability, safety, and tradition. They were designed to be very proper and slightly intimidating, creating respectable formality between customers and the tellers.

Then in the early 1970s, a group of hotshot software engineers in Cambridge developed a system called EFTS or "Electronic Fund Transfer System." This was the first successful large-scale application of computer technology to the complex and arcane world of financial transactions. The good news was that the system worked. The question was how to introduce it to a reluctant marketplace.

To help answer the question, a special team of creative consultants was assembled to meet with the software experts and banking executives from the First National City Bank (now Citicorp) in New York City. The charge was to study the implications of the new software to see how the banking industry might work differently, assuming that EFTS could gain widespread consumer acceptance. The bankers knew the software was revolutionary, but they did not know what its ultimate effects might be.

The consultants included an architect, a graphic designer and an artist. They were not experts in computer technology, banking or marketing, but were chosen for their ability to understand and imagine changes in complex systems, and then to give some visual and practical form to new ideas that could be implemented. The financial guys knew that something big was about to happen to their industry, and they knew that they needed some pretty unconventional help to figure out what it would be.

So the team went to work, holed up in a hotel with plenty of sketch paper, magic markers and coffee. Ideas flew about like quarks, bouncing off the walls, colliding and combining, disappearing and reappearing and finally coalescing. Ideas were recorded, sorted and rearranged on a gigantic roll of brown butcher paper. When the team was finished, ninety feet of ideas were presented to the bank executives.

The implications of EFTS were enormous. The design team correctly predicted the total reconfiguration of the banking industry. With the new software, checks no longer needed to be paper. In fact, money didn't need to exist at all. Banks didn't need to exist in buildings—they could be anywhere, even in a telephone. Banking was conceived to be totally accessible twenty-four hours a day, instantaneous and nearly subconscious.

Within a few years, the first ATMs started to appear in bank lobbies. People were cautious at first, but as they became accustomed to the convenience and accessibility, the machines gained popularity. The number of banking transactions exploded exponentially. The number of tellers declined sharply, even as their productivity doubled.

Pretty soon consumers stopped thinking about banks as a

place to go, and began to think about banks as a network of financial services, available whenever and wherever they wanted. Banks as buildings began to disappear and became reincarnated as vending machines.

For designers, this did not mean the end of banks as clients. Quite the contrary, it opened up a whole new set of opportunities—renovations of bank lobbies, thousands of ATM centers, new large-scale data processing centers and so forth.

What's the lesson here for designers? That technology crushes standards and can create previously unimaginable new paradigms, some doors will close and others will open. Ultimately, it is the power of ideas that rules the marketplace.

QUESTIONS

1. If this can happen for banks, what does it suggest for hospitals, libraries, offices and retail centers?

2. How do your strengths become your weaknesses, and vice versa?

3. Do you sell a product or a service? How do you know?

MANAGEMENT CHOREOGRAPHY: ORGANIZING YOUR PROJECT TEAM

> "Find your specialty—no matter how narrow it
> is—and communicate it convincingly."
>
> HARRY BECKWITH

Many designers cling to the romantic notion that great projects are constructed from flashes of brilliant insight. Creativity and inspiration are necessary, of course, but not sufficient; they are relatively useless without a lot of hard work to flesh out the details.

What design professionals can do better than anyone else is organize and choreograph the various creative and technical skills that are necessary to produce integrated results. Above all, this depends on communication and teamwork. While we may teach our young graduates that the road to success is paved with stupendous personal effort, many all-nighters and lots of caffeine, in reality, this is a misleading and harmful lesson. The truth is that success is a function of leadership and teamwork. Unless designers truly understand how to organize a team effort, the odds of professional success are slim indeed.

Ego and teamwork can be like oil and water, but this doesn't have to be the case. In fact, teams often benefit from strong egos—people who have a vision and are able to promote it passionately. Quality design depends on passion, but passion that is misused can be harmful and even destructive. In our professional careers, we have all witnessed talented people who just couldn't seem to get along with others and allowed their personal differences to poison the project or disrupt the firm.

No project runs entirely smoothly. It is the nature of the creative process to be exploratory, to look at a problem from different angles in order to develop the most appropriate solutions. Multiple perspectives can often lead to conflict, particularly if team members are in competition to "win." If winning is defined as the difference between my way and your way, then it is a zero-sum game.

However, if winning is defined as producing the best project, then every idea, every suggestion, and every person can be a contributor to overall success. In this case, winning means being the person who can do the most good for the team. There is a world of difference.

People come in different sizes, shapes, attitudes and talents. Smart leadership recognizes this and finds a way to extract the best from each and every team member according to his or her ability to contribute. Though personal dynamics can be tricky, there are a few simple principles that, if followed consistently, will guarantee better results for everyone.

1. **Separate personality from the problem.** Everybody is entitled an opinion about the right solution. However, the solution should be based on the problem, not the personalities. Legitimate differences of opinion can usually be analyzed so that decisions can be made on the basis of facts, not personal preference.

2. **Delegate to the appropriate person.** Teams are based on the premise that some members have "better" expertise than others in certain areas. This is sensible, so act accordingly. Let engineers make engineering decisions so that designers can design. If your acoustical consultant makes a strong recommendation, odds are that there is a good reason for it. Listen to your team experts—that is why you are paying them. If there is a conflict, develop an approach that no one has thought of before.

3. **Give clear, unambiguous directions.** In a well-organized team, each person has a defined role. First basemen should not attempt to play the outfield—it makes it very difficult to handle the bunts. It takes discipline to play your position so that your part of the field is covered, and it is just as important to keep out of the way and trust the other team members to play theirs. Let your team members know what you expect, why you expect it, when you expect it and how much it should cost. Then hold them to it. Reasonable directions that are consistently enforced will raise everyone's performance level and build trust in the group.

4. **Keep things in perspective.** There's a saying in academia to the effect that, "the politics are so fierce because the stakes are so small." Some things just aren't all that important to fight about. In his classic book *Up the Organization*, Robert Townsend tells the story of a heated debate about choosing the right color of coffee cups for the company cafeteria. Then it dawned on him that it would be faster and cheaper simply to make an arbitrary decision and change it later if need be. This is not to say that sloppy thinking should be tolerated, only that the level of effort

invested should be proportionate to the value of the outcome. If it's not really that important, don't worry about it; make a decision and move on to bigger and more critical things.

In today's complicated world, no project gets off the ground without a committed client, sound financing, multiple permits and approvals, defined budgets and schedules, legions of consultants, compliance with complicated codes and regulations and, by the way, good design. It takes teamwork to manage all of this, and teamwork depends on effective leadership. Seen this way, leadership is, in fact, a critical design skill.

QUESTIONS

1. How do you appreciate and expose different attitudes and talents among your staff?

2. Do you give clear directions? How do you know?

3. How do you lead? Can you also be a good follower?

MANAGING FOR SUCCESS: SYNERGIZING THE TALENT AROUND YOU

"A man's mind stretched to a new idea never goes back to its original dimensions."

OLIVER WENDELL HOLMES

One of the great joys of being a designer is seeing ideas take flight and become real products, real spaces and real places. It is a magical transition, and one that requires both enormous passion and tremendous attention to detail.

Because the design process is so personal, many designers find themselves thoroughly engrossed in it, and they have great difficulty delegating meaningful parts of the work to others. This often creates an unintentional and counterproductive impediment to good design.

Every design problem is multi-dimensional and complex and requires the blended talents of a wide variety of professionals, including architects, consultants, contractors and clients. Ironically, it is the desire for ultimate design control that is the undoing of so many designers, since no single individual, no matter how talented, can do such a complicated job entirely alone.

The trick to getting the design results you want is to take maximum advantage of the talent that lies around you. It is obvious that control is a self-limiting thing since there is a boundary to everyone's time, attention and energy. However, there is no limit to influence. Which kind of designer are you? One who's focused on control, or one who's focused on influence?

We often seek control to compensate for the fear that "nobody can do it as well as I can." A more accurate perspective would be that "nobody will do it exactly the same way I would." There is an important difference. Though all of us are talented, none of us is perfect. There is always more than one way to solve a problem and more than one way to get something done. If we allow ourselves a measure of humility, we will realize that other people will have different (and sometimes better) ways of doing things. If we are smart, we will borrow these good ideas because they will make us more effective.

If, on the other hand, we are convinced that ours is the best and only way, then we have the built-in opportunity to teach our colleagues and spread our influence. Either way, a dialogue opens up and the end result gets better. If we are restrictive and controlling in our thinking and management style, then we deny our colleagues, our clients and ourselves the advantages of leveraging many minds and creating the best design solution.

Leveraging your talent takes delegation, and effective delegation requires a leap of faith that your instructions have been understood, agreed to and will be acted upon. Sometimes this happens, and sometimes it doesn't. More often than not, the "mistakes" our colleagues make in carrying out our intentions can be directly traced to inadequate or confusing instructions in the first place. In other words, the gap in the delegation process comes from within us, not from others.

How does this play out in day-to-day practice? To delegate effectively, you need to have the full attention of your team members. They need to understand your intent, your motivation, your methods and the measure of what constitutes success. You need to provide room in the dialogue for debate, disagreement, and the new ideas that are bound to surface when different people look at a problem from different angles.

One absolute requirement for proper delegation is trust. You and your colleagues need to have a common goal uppermost in mind, and that goal is the successful completion of the project. This requires strong leadership, because when people pursue different goals or agendas, confusion and discord are inevitable.

Good leadership sets clear expectations for measurable results, establishes personal authority and responsibility for the outcome, sets the process in motion and then guides, but does not control the process. If you are confident in your abilities, then adjusting from time to time to deal with unexpected anomalies is not a big issue; rather it confirms your professionalism and sense of direction.

So, explain yourself clearly, delegate effectively, trust yourself and engage your colleagues both inside and outside the office. Abandon control in favor of influence. Being in control is temporary, at best, but being influential is the path to sustainable long-term success.

QUESTIONS

1. How can you become more trustworthy?

2. How will you take advantage of the talent around you without trying to solve everything yourself?

3. Does your staff believe that you are a delegator?

LEARNING HOW TO ASK FOR HELP

"The greatest problem with communication is
the illusion that it has been accomplished."

GEORGE BERNARD SHAW

If you're a principal, you're a leader, but are you really exercising leadership or merely authority? You get to make critical decisions about marketing, management and design, and it feels great to be in a position to get things done. You can decide which projects to chase, how to negotiate fees, who to assign to projects, how to handle key design issues, which consultants to hire and who gets promoted in your firm. Now that you're in charge, what do you need most to be successful?

The answer may surprise you. What you need most is help. As a leader, manager and mentor, your personal authority literally begins and ends at your own desk. It's useless unless you have somebody else to interact with—someone who understands what you need done and extends your influence by actually carrying out your wishes. Who are you going to lead, manage or mentor without staff, unless you enjoy talking only to the mirror? In a very real sense, authority is like an electrical circuit—it carries no current unless it is connected at both ends.

Exercising authority properly depends on three things—communication, humility and restraint—things not normally taught in design school. Communication is critical. Without it, your instructions are sure to be misunderstood and mistakenly executed, creating frustration for all concerned. Humility is equally important. Show that you respect your team members, especially your subordinates, so that they will respect you in return. Don't be fooled by the illusion of power. If you have to pull rank to get things done, it's like using too much salt—the whole dish is ruined. Use restraint. Power and authority depend as much on the receiver as the giver. You may get away with a little yelling and screaming from time to time, and it might even make you feel good, but ultimately, all it does is erode your professional standing both inside and outside the office.

The highest and best use of power is also the most subtle—it's called getting help. Getting help is the act of engaging others to assist you in accomplishing your goals. To get help, the first step is to acknowledge that you need it. This is very tough for most bosses to do. After all, you've probably spent much of your career angling up the food chain, and now that you've become a big fish, you might be shocked to discover how powerless you really are without the support of your subordinates. Surprised? Don't be. Whether you realize it or not, your subordinates are the only reason that you are a boss in the first place. Who needs a sheriff if there is no posse?

Asking for help does not mean you have suddenly become a weakling. It only means that you have finally become strong enough to understand from both a strategic and tactical perspective how to make the best use of all of your assets, and that you know how to keep your people fully engaged in furthering the firm's mission. Getting help from everybody all the time is the best way to keep the firm firing on all cylinders.

The trick is to get people to respond properly. Instead of just

shouting out orders, make sure that your colleagues understand
what you want, why you want it, when you want it and what
they can do that you are either not qualified or too busy to do.
Remember, when asked properly, people love to help. They will
eagerly take on new tasks and responsibilities if they know that
their efforts will truly make a difference. In the process, two
things will happen. Your staff will become better helpers, and
you will become a much more effective leader.

Power doesn't come from the number of merit badges you
get, but rather your ability to solve bigger and more complex
problems and to create more and more value for your clients,
your projects and your firm. Truly effective people understand
this, because they are less interested in the trappings of authority than how to exercise it wisely. Why? Because power mis-
spent dissipates quickly, whereas power used wisely compounds
with interest.

The best way to get more power is to learn how to get more
help. And to get more help, you need to learn how to be a better helper. Once you get the power, pass it along to others. If
you doubt this, try an experiment. Do an hour's worth of routine tasks entirely alone. You'll soon realize that you're wasting
precious time doing things that could be done better, faster and
cheaper by others. Then compound that by adding all of the
things you have to get done in a single day, either at home or in
the office. You will quickly see that putting yourself in a position to get the most help possible is the smartest use of your
time. Then, and only then, can you exercise your influence in
the best possible way. The wise use of power and authority is
called leadership, and it works.

QUESTIONS

1. Who has real power in your organization?

2. How is the power being used?

3. What can you do to increase your influence?

PRINCIPAL LEADERSHIP— CHOOSING THE NEXT GENERATION

"Who must do the difficult things? Those who can."

JAPANESE RIDDLE

Many an ambitious young designer has worked hard to become a firm principal, thinking that once this goal was reached, life would become simple. Adoring clients would flock to their door, awe-struck subordinates would implement every order promptly, and consultants and contractors alike would instantly follow through on all design decisions. The truth, of course, is just the opposite.

Becoming a principal means that life gets much more complicated. Rather than having only one boss at a time, a firm leader must answer to many. This includes not only external bosses (clients, bankers, reviewing agencies), but also internal bosses—the very subordinates that the principal purports to lead.

Why? Because being a firm principal means that you are responsible for the entire organization—you must find and secure work, you must hire and train the right people, you must create design that is both imaginative and practical, and you must do all this on schedule and within budget. Make no mistake about it, running a firm is not the same thing as running a project. It's the difference between playing an instrument and leading an orchestra.

Smart principals understand this. They learn how to identify the critical issues that need the most attention. They think strategically, find a way to motivate others, and delegate. If they are really smart, they also start thinking about the next generation of leadership from day one. Why? Because if they don't do this, they risk becoming the last principal that the firm will ever have.

Connecting to a Powerful Future

It is ironic but true that the best test of true leadership is how well the firm is prepared for the next generation to take over. The landscape is littered with the carcasses of many once-proud firms that have lost influence because leadership transition was not a priority.

One of the most important jobs of a principal is to make sure that there is an ample supply of talented, well-trained future leaders, at least one of whom will be able to do a much better job of running the firm than the current boss. Without an ethic of continually developing new leadership, the firm is in serious jeopardy.

How does leadership get passed from one generation to the next? Every year, a new crop of first-year students enters design school. Very few among them will emerge as leaders of their generation. Who are they? How do you spot the talent? How do you get them to work at your firm? And once you get them in the door, how do you get them to stay?

These are critical questions for any principal worth the title. Identifying, training and motivating talent is the single most important success factor for any firm regardless of size, location or market focus. Why? Because a firm is only as good as its people. If you doubt this, try producing a project without a team; it's like trying to play tennis alone.

So how do you go about finding your future leaders? First and foremost, you must be convinced that they exist, even if they are different from you. Don't look for clones no matter how tempting or flattering that may be. Each generation of a firm must respond to different pressures and opportunities, and it is very likely that tomorrow's leaders will need different skills. Instead, look for values. In any talent pool, find the top 10 percent—those who will find a way to rise to the top like bubbles in champagne.

The Ideal Candidate

The ideal candidate may not be obvious at first. Future leaders come in all sizes, shapes and backgrounds, but they do share some common characteristics. Foremost among these are curiosity, the ability to deal with people and the ability to hold attention. Curious people never stop learning. They read, they attend seminars, they bug you about new ideas, they participate in professional committees, they develop new skills, and they bring their enthusiasm with them to the office. For them, the line between the personal life and the professional life is a fuzzy one, and they find a way to integrate the two. They see their professional careers as a lifelong commitment.

Curious types tend to have good people skills because they are interested in the world around them and what makes it tick. They have the ability to see more than one point of view at a time and to understand conflict from a variety of perspectives without being judgmental. They recognize that everyone has value to offer and that the trick is to figure out what that might be and then engage it in a productive way. They may be passionate or opinionated, but they are also tolerant. They respect the feelings of others even when they don't agree with them on every point. They know when to be politically expedient without compromising their core values. In short, they are inclusive, not exclusive, thinkers.

Regenerative Interdependence

The combination of curiosity, consideration and commitment creates a leadership style that holds attention. When there is a project meeting, a client presentation or an office conference, pay attention to whose words and actions affect the outcome. Personal style is not the issue here. Rather it is the ability to be an impact player, one who can articulate a sense of direction for the group. It doesn't necessarily take great oratory to move a crowd.

Sometimes a quiet comment or a perceptive question will do the job. While some people might strive for attention, others will concentrate on the results. There is a big difference between the two. Pay attention to those in your firm who think clearly and produce the goods, because those are the people that your clients will be paying attention to.

Once you have found your acorns, nurture them until they become oak trees. Challenge them with new assignments. Encourage them to get involved in community activities where they will meet many different kinds of people. Send them to seminars and conferences and expect a full report and a presentation to the firm when they return. Encourage them to take chances, and be tolerant of their mistakes. This will increase both confidence and humility at the same time—a most powerful combination.

Finally, teach them to teach others. Make sure that the ethic of passing the baton of leadership doesn't stop with you or with them but is embedded in the next generation down the line as part of the firm's value system. Actively promoting the growth of new leaders from within and giving away power might seem like a dangerous thing to do, but in fact it is the only safe path to the future. Bottom line, when your successors are successful, so are you.

QUESTIONS

1. How are you preparing the next generation to lead?

2. How do you challenge future principals with new assignments?

3. Are you afraid of "delegating yourself out of a job"?

CRITICISM VS. LEADERSHIP

"Just as there is management unwilling or unenlightened enough to accept good design, there are designers who are only too willing to accommodate them."

PAUL RAND

How do firms thrive? Why do some grow and others wither? What does it take to be successful in a constantly changing world? While we may hope for a secret formula or a foolproof organization chart or a magic key to unlock these mysteries, the truth is that there is no mystery at all. The answer to the question is simple and straightforward: firms thrive because of their people.

A successful firm is a place that attracts and retains talented staff and then provides an environment in which they can do their very best work. Good people love a challenge, they love to learn, and they love to work with colleagues who will push them to achieve more than they thought they could. How do you go about making sure your staff is as committed as you are to the success of the operations?

First and foremost, recognize that each and every person comes to work with some kind of talent. As a leader, it is your job to unlock that talent and get it into gear. To do this, you need to be candid with your employees about what you expect from them, how they can contribute to the organization, and how you see their growth potential.

More importantly, you need to be honest with yourself. It is not unusual for senior management to have an inflated self-image and subscribe to the notion that "nobody can do it as well as I can." While this might be true in isolated cases, it should also be a strong signal that you need to find and train somebody who can do a particular task better, faster or cheaper than you can. Why? Leverage. Don't waste your time doing things that can be delegated. Instead, find a way of training and promoting your people and helping them to grow. This will free you to do a better job in the areas that really matter.

When you delegate, mistakes will be made—that's the nature of the learning process. Remember that you can delegate authority but not responsibility. If something goes wrong, you are on the hook, but don't let this stop you. Delegation most often goes awry when the subordinate did not clearly understand the task at hand. Another way of saying this is that the delegator—that's you—failed to make the instructions properly understood.

When you delegate, you are first and foremost a teacher. Because things are never perfect, you will be tempted to criticize way too much. The first reaction, which is a very human one, is to react negatively (as in "that's not good enough"). When you react this way, you miss an important opportunity to demonstrate humility—a powerful teaching tool. Remember that there was a time in your life when you would have gotten it wrong, too. There was a time when you didn't know much, made stupid mistakes and relied on the help of others to get through the day. So lighten up. Share your failures to make a point.

Criticism is often used as a weapon to demonstrate that "I am smarter than you and I want you and everybody else to know it." This causes more problems for the critic than one might realize. Unjust or excessive criticism only makes the critic look silly and diminishes their credibility. Too much ranting and raving can cause deafness in the audience. Do you really want a leadership style based on intimidation? To keep your credibility high, use your comments to enlighten, not to perish. And remember to give praise in public, but to criticize in private.

Ultimately, if you understand how important your staff is to your success, you'll use your leadership skills to reinforce continuous learning. You'll share your knowledge and experience generously. And you'll be astounded at the reaction. There is no leverage like the leverage of teamwork. A selfish or critical management style places a chokehold on the organization, but a truly wise leader takes as much joy in the success of others as in personal success. Know the difference between criticism and leadership. It will determine whether your firm will thrive or merely survive.

QUESTIONS

1. How can you share your failures to strengthen the firm?

2. Are you a leader or a critic? How do you know?

ARE YOU A FISH OR
A THERMOSTAT?

*"When an organization becomes productive,
it gains control of its destiny."*

JACK WELSH

E ven in the best of times, the enterprise of design is fraught with frustrations—how to attract the right clients, how to negotiate sufficient fees, how to hire and retain talented staff, how to make sure that projects are well designed yet still run on time and on budget. Given the pressures and the variables in making good architecture, it should come as no surprise that there is more than one way to address each of these questions. However, success, like design itself, is not an accident—it is largely a matter of choice.

What are the critical ingredients of success in a design firm? To some, marketing is paramount because in order to produce a project, the firm must win it first. To others, the key is innovative design and the creation of new and interesting solutions. For the pragmatic, the production process matters most—the nitty gritty of getting the work done and making sure that all of the details are in order. Some believe that good management is most important—making sure that all the policies, procedures and numbers are in order so that things can run smoothly. The truth, of course, is that all these things are essential. It takes leadership to establish the balance.

Every person has a leadership style. Some see themselves like

Teddy Roosevelt, leading the cavalry charge up San Juan Hill. They tend to be energetic, enthusiastic and egocentric. They like to attract attention, inspire others, and they often measure their success by how much they "win." Others are more like chessmasters—they survey the entire board and try to find a way to use all the pieces at their disposal in a coordinated way. They understand the choreography of the grand strategy and are willing to sacrifice on a small issue if the greater good is served. Either way, success depends on effective leadership.

Consider "success" in an aquarium. Some people might imagine themselves as the fish—brightly colored, with interesting and exotic shapes, full of movement, and the focus of attention. However, the fish are lost in their own context. A fish in water doesn't even realize that it's wet. They might compete with other fish for food or attention, but they can't control their environment—they can only contend with it. "Success" for the fish is really just a matter of survival.

Ironically, success in the aquarium does not depend on the fish at all, but rather on the thermostat. Whatever the size, number, species or survival skill of the fish, the temperature of the water is all-powerful—a variation of only a few degrees either way will determine which fish will flourish and which will flounder. While the power of the thermostat may not be obvious to the visitor, in the aquarium it is all pervasive.

Consider your own leadership style. Is pride of authorship important? Can you willingly (and gratefully) accept useful suggestions? Can you inspire others to action without getting in their way? Do you confuse criticism with leadership? Do you know how to delegate effectively, taking delight in the success of others in your firm as they learn how to achieve their own

goals? Can you provide strong and clear direction without stifling those around you?

Successful leaders understand the subtleties of these questions. *They realize that in order for the fish to thrive, somebody has
to work the thermostat.* Design is a multi-faceted enterprise that
requires the skilled contributions not only of architects but also
of clients, consultants, and contractors. Even the most talented
among us need a great deal of help to do a good job. By con-
centrating on the big picture, you can gain maximum advantage
of all the talent at your disposal—especially if some of it's not
your own.

Some people are made to be fish, and they require a support
system for survival. Others are thermostats, more conductors
than soloists. Which are you? Understanding your leadership
style, and how it affects those around you, will help you make
success a choice, not an accident.

QUESTIONS

1. What is your leadership style—are you a fish or a thermostat?

2. How can you make sure that all your "fish" say healthy?

3. What is the right balance of criticism and encouragement?

DON'T DROP THE PROFIT BALL

> "Dryness promotes the formation of flower
> buds...flowering is, after all, not an aesthetic
> contribution, but a survival mechanism."
>
> ANN HAYMOND ZWINGER

Design organizations must become better run businesses. It is their number one strategic concern.
Professional firms that survive and prosper are differ-
entiated from others by the unique advantages they possess in
marketing, service delivery, design talent, professional competence and integrity. And the management structure of the firm is
the framework that supports and advances these qualities.
Fundamentally, the competitive advantage that a firm has earned
must be managed to stay fresh, attractive and agile.

Managing a successful firm is a lot like being a juggler who is
trying to keep five balls in the air. Four of the balls are red and
only one of the balls is black. The red balls represent marketing,
money, people, and services. The black ball represents profit. No
matter what happens, the black ball should never be dropped. Of
course, most firm principals understand that they cannot exist
without profits; however, the importance of profit often gets lost
in the midst of exciting marketing victories, sexy design solutions, and responding to those urgent client demands that are
daily occurrences.

Firms cannot hire someone else to be responsible for their

profitability. Only the principals of the firm can be accountable
for protecting profits. They must be the leaders and role models
for others to follow. It makes simple sense—but it's not particularly
common except in the best-run firms. Leadership is
the very heart and soul of business management. A firm's success
is complicated, but what is ultimately understood by all
those who fail is that cash, profits, and trying to become a
"best-of-class firm" are all vitally important components in a
firm's culture.

It is still a sobering thought that far too many design firms
and organizations are under-performing cash traps. To achieve
success in the future, begin with a strong business plan and a
resolve to be an effective manager of people. Profits are sure to
follow.

QUESTIONS

1. How will you stay fresh, attractive, and agile?

2. Leaders are responsible and accountable for maximizing
   productivity. What is your track record?

3. How do you communicate your attitude about good business
   practices in your firm?

LEADING A HEALTHY ORGANIZATION

"Norman Foster's most important characteristic, the one that won him the reputation he coveted, was his ability to change."

DESIGNINTELLIGENCE

Times change, and when they do, intelligent firms know how to stay resilient. They know that markets can and will decline. Land values can and will fluctuate. Capital investments can and will vary. Traditional opportunities to build backlogs can and will decline. How do smart firms stay healthy? Here are five strategies to keep you organizationally fit and resilient.

1. **A communications plan is as important as a marketing plan.** Both internally and externally, a good plan includes mission, vision, messages, audiences, techniques, schedules, budget, implementation, and monitoring systems. Best-of-class firms have a communications plan, and they know that it not only keeps them healthy, it also gives them more bounce and resiliency when the downturn comes. They don't forget that a design firm is in the communications business.

2. **Structure your marketing budgets for results.** Advertise in the appropriate venues. Have a high profile at client trade shows. Have at least twelve communication events

per year. Use creative methods to connect with key audiences. Successful firms are positioned, enthusiastic, and ready to take away work from other less aggressive competitors. Marketing plans are a part of the overall communications plan.

3. **Use technology.** Automate everything. Have a technology plan. Update your Web site every month. Use the latest CAD technology. Use portable phones with a passion so you are never out of touch.

4. **Keep overhead low and have a corporate culture of innovation.** Have a business plan that includes culture and image. Bring clients and prospective clients to the firm most every day. Make the firm an incubator for imagination, creativity, and new solutions for your clients' real life problems. Showcase low overhead solutions, keep fixed expenses down, and keep the work environment fresh, clean, organized and exciting. "Walk the walk" and "talk the talk" of good design. Know how to be profitable by design.

5. **Have a leadership plan.** Running a successful firm is not just about cash flow, bringing in good people, getting work, keeping billable time up and getting bills and taxes paid. Firms need leadership that is energized, confident and caring. This will empower the staff: they'll have tools and they'll have a coach. They not only know the vision but they know that each individual is important in the firm. Have a succession plan for the CEO. The staff should know they have a future with the firm, and they should look forward to being a shareholder.

A new world of design and intellectual capital is unfolding at a staggering pace. It stands to reason those firms with the best business skills and best design talent will have a market advantage.

In our work with organizations, publications, and firms, we have discovered a profile of today's successful design firm. The following five characteristics are those most often mentioned by firms that are successful and satisfied today:

1. **Developing a coherent point of view about the future.** No firm outperforms its aspirations, so they should be very high: expansive and motivating.

2. **Operating with a vision and a plan.** Most often this includes a few non-linear futures inventions. Their business plan is most often edgy—it doesn't just rely on last year's success formula.

3. **Extinguishing inertia in their organizations.** They co-opt and neutralize the anti-change forces within their ranks.

4. **Using a vocabulary of action and motivation.** They are not held back by binary opposites; instead they build bridges using unifying business logic.

5. **Focusing on priorities and accountability.** They are disciplined toward renewing their goals and achieving them.

There are new problems and solutions ahead. Firms should ready themselves now for what's coming. The market prospects will dim in some sectors and shine in others. Yet, design leaders can put the fundamentals in place and use their unique talents, skills, energy, and enthusiasm to design a better future for themselves.

1. How have you created a feeling of urgency for change?

2. What are the forces resisting change in your firm?

3. Is your vision challenging, easy to understand, and capable of evolving over time?

USING BINARY LOGIC

> "Why is this firm dead? Why is it only an
> organization chart and a set of financials?
> Where do we measure its connections with
> people, with clients, with partners?"
>
> DAVID FIRTH

T his is a story about meeting the expectations of clients and audiences. Our story is based on observation in two design organizations—an architecture firm and an industrial design firm. Visits to these firms gave us a new perception into their internal working environments. We saw exceptional talent and awesome projects. The potential for professional satisfaction was very high. Yet there was an underlying weakness—the principals/partners are not synergizing well and are not getting along with each other.

In these two examples there is a negative, permeating stress—an unspoken binary opposition exists among key principals that under cuts these firms' self-esteem, communications, morale, and leadership. The differences between the leaders in the organizations are taking on a weight of opposition rather than a new knowledge sharing. Diversity can strengthen, but some firms behave in ways that allow diversity to become a weakness.

Logically, it follows that how well a firm gets along internally determines how well it performs externally. Value in a firm lives where there is applied knowledge that meets clients' needs.

Harmonious leadership can then become an asset of the firm's culture. A firm's intangible assets are established by their leaders' actions.

Binary logic gives structure to a firm's culture and services— manifested through its behavior and knowledge management. When a firm's leaders are involved in ideological conflict, it can lead to creative opposition that can energize it toward a new level of competitive fitness. For example, a principal can find a unifying logic in these seemingly opposites:

The duel becomes "The Duo."

- Exterior vs. Interior *becomes* Architecture and Interior Design
- Design vs. Business *becomes* Design Enterprise
- Design vs. Construction *becomes* Design-Build

Sometimes firm principals argue for ideological positions that hold a binary position to another principal for dubious reasons. This can be just pure gamesmanship. This influences the firm's culture—often leading to stress, dysfunction, and high turnover.

Delivering value is difficult enough without the stresses of an organization's leaders not getting along. Yet, when they do get along, the rewards are numerous—and can be measured. In these cases, the binary opposites are transformed into positive values that permeate the firm's culture. The client then receives service value that is synergistic with the firm's culture and talent. The phrase "we exceed expectations" can be the new reality and makes "getting along" the intelligent thing to do. Finding the unifying logic in binary opposites and creating harmony is one of today's most ignored, yet powerful leadership differentiators.

1. Are your firm's principals in alignment with each other?

2. How can you challenge the status-quo in your firm without being oppositional?

3. What can you do to create more effective team work among senior management?

DESIGN BY DEMOGRAPHICS

> "Our 'secret formula' is actually not very formulaic. It's a blend of methodologies, work practices, culture, and infrastructure."
>
> TOM KELLEY

All design firms, whatever their size, location or market focus, have one thing in common: They are made up entirely of people. Like instruments in an orchestra, it is the people who determine the substance and tone of the organization. They come in all sizes and shapes, with different backgrounds, training, and talent opinions about what's really important.

Try this experiment. Pull five people aside at random and ask them each to describe your firm in a few sentences. Chances are you'll get five very different answers. Since not only your firm but all of the organizations your firm deals with (including clients, contractors, and consultants) are also made up of people, it pays to understand the overlooked but powerful role that demographics play in shaping any organization.

To understand your demographics, determine how many staff you have by age, sex, educational background, number of years with the firm, compensation level, work experience, and so forth. With this knowledge, you'll be able to track the stages of professional growth that all of them will encounter in the course of their careers. Understanding this will help you deal with the behavioral aspects of managing your firm successfully and especially in how you put together project teams.

In general, there are four stages of professional growth—1) learning, 2) doing, 3) leading and, 4) teaching. The learners are the young Turks who can't wait to change the world. They are enthusiastic and passionate, curious and inquisitive, and what they lack in knowledge or experience is made up by youthful energy. The really smart learners quickly discover that there's a lot they don't know. They may be the lowest on the totem pole, but they have the most potential because their future has not yet been determined.

It usually takes about three to five years to pass through the learner stage to the "doer" stage. By this time, a person realizes that the "real world" is infinitely more complex than the ivory tower—real clients have real budgets and schedules and have to contend with dozens of complex issues in the course of producing a project.

Things aren't so black and white, and the passion of the learner is tempered by the political reality of getting things done in a team setting. During the doer stage, the employee usually concentrates on developing a specific skill set. Is he or she best suited to design, management, production, marketing or perhaps construction administration? This is a critical stage because the path that is chosen will shape their longer-term career development.

The doers who successfully demonstrate their competence will become leaders of teams, projects, and eventually, of firms. By this time they have learned how to parlay their specific skills, which may in fact be quite specialized or limited, into much broader leadership qualities. As their judgment matures, they are seen as problem solvers, and they understand the difference between strategy and tactics.

Emerging leaders also understand the power of leverage. They realize that they cannot do everything by themselves and that they need the right kind of help to accomplish a larger goal. The willingness to seek and accept help is one of the hallmarks of a good leader.

The leadership phase can last for many years, and some people actually stop growing when they have assumed a position of authority, mistakenly thinking that they have "arrived." However, the truly wise do not stop there. Understanding the difference between control and influence, they realize that the greatest power of all is the power to shape the next generation. This is when they become teachers.

Good teachers don't stop learning, doing or leading. Even while in a position of authority, good leaders are concerned about developing the next generation. They consciously seek out promising younger talent, becoming mentors. If they are smart, they always hire people who are smarter. Being both clever and wise, they realize that their success absolutely depends upon the people around them. The influence of a good teacher extends throughout the entire organization from top to bottom, and the values that are transmitted are long lasting. It only takes a few good teachers to make a tremendous difference.

To better understand your organization, try charting some basic statistics. Take a look at the number of staff by chronological age, years of experience with the firm, compensation level and phase of professional development. You'll quickly see what patterns emerge and where the gaps are. When you add staff, the demographic profile will help you hire strategically; you'll be able to match the strength of the candidate to the true needs of the organization. The charts will also help with managing your professional development.

It will not only help you with management; it will help your staff understand their individual roles in the organization and what the potential for growth is. Do you have too many designers, or not enough? Do the numbers show that you have too much turnover, or too little? Are you paying too much or too little for talent and experience? Has the time come to consider adding new partners? These are only a few of the issues that demographic analysis will raise. How you address them will determine your success.

QUESTIONS

1. How can you reinforce the four stages of professional growth—learning, doing, leading and teaching?

2. Do you hire people who are smarter than you?

3. What does your firm's demographic profile tell you?

FIRE IN THE BELLY: TOTAL PRINCIPAL COMMITMENT

"The idea is to assign yourself responsibility for being a motivator and an innovator."

I.M. PEI

One of the myths about being an architect is that once you make principal, your troubles are over. As a leader, you expect loyalty and obedience from staff. As a professional, you expect a certain deference from consultants and clients. As a citizen, you expect the respect of the community at large. The truth, however, is quite different. None of these things happens automatically just because you get a new business card.

On the other hand, some principals are working an average of sixty-five hours a week, cutting their bonuses to make up for inefficient project managers and are also required to market, network, manage and serve as referee, therapist and parent. Many of those in ownership positions are asking themselves, "Why would I aspire to such a position?"

Making principal means that your life gets harder, more complicated, more hectic and more challenging. Your responsibilities have increased exponentially. Instead of being concerned about a single project or client, you are now expected to be a provider, creating new work for the office, mentoring the staff and producing results for your clients, not to mention keeping the bank happy by covering payroll every two weeks. Being a principal is hard work. It is a position of great responsibility, and it carries commensurate professional, financial and psychological rewards.

Becoming a principal is one thing. Maintaining the energy, commitment and enthusiasm that got you there in the first place is quite another. In sports, it is very common for a championship team to have an off season the following year, because the emotional and physical energy that is required to win is even harder to sustain. The same thing is true in architecture. It is not uncommon for principals in firms, especially those nearing retirement, to do a little coasting. After all, they've "earned it." Shorter work weeks, longer vacations and longer lunches become the norm rather than the exception. While it is certainly true that exceptional performance should have its rewards, it is very dangerous for the firm to allow anybody at any level to slack off. This is especially true of principals, because they set the tone for the entire organization. If the principals are not giving their all, who will?

How do you make sure that the principals in your firm continue to perform at the peak of their ability? How do you keep the fire in the belly from going out? The answers to these questions are complicated by the fact that design firms are too often a club rather than a business.

Partnership is not only a measure of professional achievement, it is also an affinity group. Each member is likely to bring different skills and attitudes to the mix, and establishing equal performance measures for all can be dangerous. At the same time, ignoring principal performance measures is asking for trouble, because when a firm loses its momentum, it is exceedingly hard to recapture.

256   Obviously, the most important time to discuss principal performance is when new partners are brought in. This is an opportunity for the entire group to reaffirm what it means to be a leader and to renew everyone's personal commitment to the overall success of the office. The key is to focus not on what you get, but what you give.

While every firm is different, there are some standards that can be reasonably applied to measure principal performance. As discussed earlier, the four critical success factors in any firm are marketing (obtaining new work), operations (establishing a productive working environment), professional services (creating and producing design), and finance (managing the money). Firms can be driven by any one of these factors, but each and every successful firm will need leadership in all of the areas in order to thrive.

Normally, firms that are not sole proprietorships should average one principal for every ten to twelve staff members, and at least $125,000 in net fees per staff. On this basis, a principal can be reasonably expected to produce no less than $2 million dollars in new fees annually. In larger firms with more sophisticated marketing support, $3 million to $5 million per principal per year is an achievable goal.

On the professional side, principals should be expected to produce their projects on time and within budget, setting an example for others. Performance can also be measured by the number of design awards won, number of projects published and the amount of repeat business generated by satisfied clients.

In operations, team building, training of younger staff and attention to routine details such as filling out time sheets and checking project reports are minimum standards, whether or not the principal is involved in direct firm management. Principals should always support firm management and be alert to new ideas about how to run the office more efficiently.

Finally, in finance, it is easy to measure project performance. How many dollars of gross fees were billed in a year? How much in net fees? What were the profit margins on specific projects? What is the average utilization of principal time? What is the ratio of new fee dollars generated per dollar of salary? It is easy to tabulate these results for all principals in the firm and then compare them on a year-to-year basis, looking for trends. The numbers themselves won't prove anything, but at the same time, objective measures of principal performance are hard to deny. Use them for enlightenment, not punishment.

If your firm tolerates less than full commitment by its principals, everyone in the firm gets sold short. This includes not only internal staff, but your clients, consultants and contractors as well. As principals near retirement age, their interests and value to the firm may change—it's perfectly understandable. When this happens, don't get mad. Instead, get creative about restructuring their involvement so that you can take advantage of what they do have to offer.

Principal performance is the single most important requirement for overall firm success, so take full advantage of it.

QUESTIONS

1. How do you evaluate principals in the firm?

2. How are your principals held accountable?

3. What steps will you take to increase principal productivity?

A STRATEGY FOR WINNING

A STRATEGY FOR WINNING

"If one advances confidently in the direction of his dreams, and endeavors to live the life which he has imagined, he will meet with success unexpected in common hours…If you have built castles in the air, your work need not be lost; that is where they should be. Now put the foundations under them."

HENRY DAVID THOREAU

Making good architecture is a complicated enterprise. It requires not only the ability to conceptualize and give physical form to the aspirations of the client, but also the management skill to organize and "choreograph" the activities of a multitude of team members, each of whom has a special contribution to make. Ideas alone do not make a building. The architect's drawings and models are only the recipe—not the meal.

Like music, design depends on both objects and processes. A piano by itself does not make music. Without the composer to write the score and a musician to play the notes, a piano is just a piece of expensive furniture. So it is with design. The essential message of *How Firms Succeed* is that understanding why and how things get done is a necessary first step in doing them better. It's a complex business, to be sure, but that should not stop us from rearranging the parts and pieces for better effect.

Watson and Crick discovered that all the infinite complexity and subtlety of human life comes from only four essential instructions encoded in our DNA. The same principle applies to design. The possibilities of design are limitless, but they are based on just a few fundamentals. In running a design enterprise, the four essentials are *marketing* (getting the work), *operations* (organizing the work), *professional services* (doing the work) and *finance* (managing the money). Any firm, regardless of its location, size, or area of specialty, needs all four to survive and thrive.

Like the gears in a car's transmission, each of the four might be a different size, but they are all interconnected and they are all necessary to make the car go. Eliminate one, and the transmission goes dead. At the same time, a gear that has too many teeth to mate properly with its neighbors does damage. For the design engine to work, the gears must be the right size, properly connected, and well lubricated. When viewed in this way, it's easy to understand why even the smallest part in the engine has a critical role to play.

This is why there are no unimportant people and no unimportant processes in your design firm. As the leader, your role is to be the "downfield blocker"—clear a path so your staff can do their best work. Beware the temptation to focus only on the big problems. To be truly effective, learn to break the big issues down into smaller, digestible chunks—the "speed bumps" that get in the way. Then take action, one issue at a time. This is the surest way to establish a culture of continuous learning and continuous improvement in your firm. It's also the quickest way to unlock the potential of all the talent at your disposal.

John Wooden, the extraordinarily successful basketball coach at UCLA, won more national championships than any other coach in the history of the game. He understood the power of simple lessons. The story goes that the first practice each year was devoted entirely to teaching the new players how to put on their socks and shoes properly. That's all they did—they put on and took off their sneakers over and over again until they got it "right." Why? Coach Wooden knew that if a player developed a blister, even a small one, he would be distracted on the court, and this could affect the team's performance. He also knew that, like design, basketball is a team sport. It didn't matter who did the scoring as long as the team won the game. Did this mean that the UCLA team lacked stars? Hardly—they attracted the very best players in the country, they performed at the peak of their abilities, and won national championships year after year. But it was Coach Wooden's simple lessons that unlocked their potential and made it possible for the stars to play as a team. This is the power of leadership.

When architects and designers truly understand their potential as leaders as well as conceptualizers and designers, their influence can only increase. But in order to be seen by others as leaders, they must first see *themselves* in that way. They must understand how to apply the full range of their design skills effectively, and this requires far more than just drawing lines on paper. They must also find ways to enable others to participate effectively in the design process, and this includes not only colleagues, but clients, consultants and contractors as well. And let's not forget the public—the ultimate consumer of all this effort. The essential act of leadership is to unleash the power of the team. In this way, design can be embraced by all who are touched by it.

We live in a technology-rich age. CAD systems make it much simpler to depict complex spatial arrangements, and e-mail, voice mail, and faxes have made instant communications ubiquitous. There is software for project budgeting and scheduling to keep things on track, and exquisitely detailed models can be constructed from laser-cut parts. The profession is rich in new tools, but it still clings to an outdated self-image, and this needs to change. Architects are not the victims of tight budgets—they are the problem solvers who can show clients how to get the best value for the resources available. Architects are not the victims of building codes or zoning regulations—they are the interpreters who know how to unlock the true potential of any site. And architects need not be the caboose on the development train—they can and should be helping to drive the locomotive. When architects see themselves as the leaders that they can be, and behave accordingly, there will be no limit to their success.

While this book contains plenty of pragmatic information about how to enhance your own "design enterprise," its essential message is about *attitude*. We are fortunate to live in an age in which design really matters. From the smallest, simplest products like Post-it Notes to major cultural institutions like the new Guggenheim Museum in Bilbao, people everywhere are beginning to understand the power of good design to make things look better, work better, last longer, and raise our spirits. Winston Churchill's observation that "first we shape our buildings, and then they shape us" is quite true, and it has been said that our buildings are the residue of our culture—the evidence we leave behind to tell the next generation what has been important to us and why. If so, it's clear that architects, engineers, and all designers can (and should) be cultural leaders, political leaders, business leaders, and educational leaders. To do this will require a new way of looking at design and design-ers. Essentially, we are in the leadership business, and design is our medium.

The time has come to redesign design—to discard the archaic preconceptions that have hindered the effectiveness and affected the self-image of the design professions. The time has come to redesign our processes, protocols and proce-dures—discarding the ones that simply don't work very well, and inventing new ones that will. The time has come to take action. This is where you come in. Benjamin Franklin wrote that "all the great maxims have been written; it only remains to put them into practice." He was right. Everything you imag-ine is possible.

aggregation: Making otherwise scattered information accessible at single or multiple locations, usually via project management web sites.

archetype: An underlying process that determines the form of imagery and symbolism, although not necessarily its content.

asynchronous innovation work: Remote software-based interaction allowing people to think, experiment, create, and contribute when they are most able (James Brian Quinn).

backlog: The amount of fee remaining in a firm at any given time. Also referred to as "fuel in the tank."

balanced scorecard (BSC): A measurement system that balances financial value and non-financial value, including design. A balanced scorecard is typically divided into a number, usually between three and six, of focus areas that have been identified as critical for the company. The focus areas are populated with indicators that are measured. Suitable for communication around and visualization of value creation. The term was coined by Robert S. Kaplan and David P. Norton.

balanced scorecard grid: A grid used for transforming the firm's strategy into measurable objectives, indicators and actions. The corporate strategy is divided into value creating focus areas of the balanced scorecard. Critical success factors are identified for strategic objectives within each focus area. Indicators are assigned to critical success factors to map the extent to which they are achieved. Actions that affect indicators are identified.

benchmarking: A continuous process of measuring and comparing outcomes, services, and processes with those that are "best-of-class." The 10 categories of best-of-class lead to "best practice."

best option: What generates the best outcome in the future. Relates to valuation of opportunities (future possible operations) (Timothy A. Luehrman).

best practice: What has generated best outcome in the past.

binary opposition: An analytic category from structuralism, used to show how meanings can be generated out of two-term systems. Meaning is generated by opposition. The binary opposition is the most extreme form of significant difference possible. Such binaries are a feature of culture not nature; they are products of signifying systems, and function to structure our perceptions of the natural and social world into order and meaning.

blueprint: A master plan for the realization of a vision.

book value: Defined as total assets minus total liabilities and represents the stockholders' equity on the firm's balance sheet. Book value is easy to determine but tends to understate the real value of the firm because assets are valued at cost less depreciation and no provision is made for the worth of the firm as a growing concern.

business process: Various related activities aimed at creating value which customers perceive and are willing to pay for.

buttress: A projection from a leader or a system of management that creates additional strength and support to an organization.

choice: "Where there's choice, there's meaning" is a basic precept in design communication.

client capital: The value of customer base, customer relationships and client potential. Component of structural capital.

client focus: The markets' and clients' perspectives on the business. A group of indicators and ratios describing the client base and relationships.

client potential: Relationships with new clients in established and new markets.

client relationship: current and potential business relationships with previous and present clients.

clients lost: The number of contracts lost during the year in relation to the total number of assignments on record.

cognitive dissonance: A state of disharmony, inconsistency or conflict between the organized attitudes, beliefs and values within an individual's cognitive system.

commercial competence: Designers' ability to collaborate with clients and other consulting partners in value creating constellations.

community of practice: A basis for collaboration in the execution of real work, based on a common sense of purpose and a real need to know what each other knows. Developed by the Institute of Learning.

competence: Encompasses knowledge, will, and skill, including professional, social, and commercial ability.

competence alliance: A network of individuals/units/firms with various competence profiles.

competence network: Organized network with a common goal of individual competence development within a certain area. Activities include sharing of information, ideas and experiences as well as a transfer of knowledge to members of the network. The core of the network is the interpersonal connections.

consensus: A term used to imply shared agreement.

contactivity: A meeting that goes beyond connectivity and creates both contact and meeting of minds leading to activity (Leif Edvinsson).

core competence: Competence that is of strategic importance for the firm's business logic.

core process: Value creating processes of strategic importance for the firm's business logic. Sometimes thought of as a "trade secret" because of unique value that some firms' processes contain.

corporate (organizational) memory: The organization's ability to transform and add experiences to the structural capital. The ability to recall, remembering what is needed when it is needed; Animated memory that supports the business processes: without stifling the innovation (Bob Johansen).

culture: The combined sum of the individual opinions, shared mindsets, values and norms (Hubert Saint-Onge). A component of organizational capital.

Economic Value Added (EVA)™: Value added that an operation generates during a certain period after deducting all costs, including capital costs for all invested or borrowed capital. Trademark owned by Stern Stewart & Company.

empiricism: An approach emphasizing the importance of observable, measurable and quantifiable evidence.

Employee Stock Ownership Plan (ESOP): An Employee Stock Ownership Plan is a type of employee benefit called a "defined contribution" plan. A fixed schedule of benefits determines what each employee will receive upon retirement, and this amount is guaranteed under the terms of the plan. The employer is then obligated to contribute what is necessary to provide these benefits.

fair market value: The price at which a business would change hands between a willing buyer and a willing seller, both being adequately informed of the relevant facts, and neither being under any compulsion to buy or sell.

fair value: Certain state statutes define value for the purpose of establishing dissenting stockholder rights. These definitions are much less clear, typically using the term "fair value" instead of "fair market value." There is no universally accepted definition of fair value. This leads to litigation on dissenting stockholder rights issues.

Gestalt: The recognition of wholeness and overall form rather than of individual component elements. An understanding of all the parts within any given structure will not provide a complete understanding of the total structure. Instead, meaning derives from the interrelationships of those parts, and of each part of the whole.

globalization: The growth and acceleration of economic and cultural networks which operate on a worldwide scale and basis.

goodwill: There are generally two types of goodwill: personal goodwill (often referred to as professional goodwill) and business goodwill (often referred to as practice goodwill). Personal goodwill is the goodwill associated with the individual. Business goodwill is the value of a business over and above its identifiable assets less liabilities.

human capital: The accumulated value of investments in employee training, competence, and future. The term focuses on the value of what the individual can produce; human capital thus encompasses individual value in an economic sense (Gary S. Becker). Can be described as the employees' competence, relationship ability and values. Work on human capital often focuses on transforming individual into collective competence and more enduring organizational capital.

human capital index: An index that indicates employees' attitudes regarding competence, motivation, responsibility and authority, cooperation and organizational efficiency.

human focus: The employee perspective. A group of indicators and ratios describing individual and collective competence and capabilities.

IC: For *intellectual capital*. The consolidation of structural capital and human capital, indicating future earnings capability. A concept developed by Leif Edvinsson.

IC leadership: The bridge between human capital, organizational capital and customer capital. Creates congruence and multiplicative effects between strategies, structures, systems and cultures in the business, market and operating environment in which an organization works.

icon/iconic: Type of sign in which there is a marked physical or perceptual resemblance between the signifier and that for which it stands.

image: Commonly means a public impression created to appeal to the audience. It may be false or authentic, and is part of brand repute.

indicator: A measurement that visualizes a certain aspect of the organization that has been identified having an impact as a key success factor. Indicators have the purpose of indicating a certain development and not to describe a target value.

information management (IM): The process of synthesizing, structuring and making information accessible.

innovation: The capacity to create a new idea or way. There are two types of innovation: one in the form of improving already existing products or services and the other in the form of creating totally new products and services.

Innovation often includes three stages: invention, translation and commercialization. Innovative firms have reason to charge higher fees.

intellectual asset: Intangible asset more closely related to brain power. Sometimes referred to as applied brilliance. It is a leadership quality but does not stand up well on its own in terms of leadership.

intellectual property: Intellectual assets that qualify for legal and commercial protection, i.e. patents, trademarks, copyrights, and trade secrets.

invention: Power of inventing or being invented. Ingenuity or creativity. Something originating in an experiment.

key performance indicator (KPI): A particular ratio or characteristic used to measure output or outcome. KPIs are "metrics of value."

key success factor (KSF): Factors that are essential in order to achieve the strategic objectives/vision statements. Critical value drivers. Best-of-class firms understand how KSFs differentiate them from traditional firms.

knowledge: Information that has value in the interaction with human capital. The ability people have to use information to solve complex problems and adapt to change. The individual ability to master the unknown. The ability to act (Karl Erik Sveiby). Knowledge can be classified as explicit or tacit (Ikujiro Nonaka).

knowledge cafe: A metaphor alluding to the fact that knowledge workers might not work at the office but in an open inviting environment, like a café. A knowledge recipe for the workplace of tomorrow for knowledge workers.

knowledge exchange: The new arena on Internet for exchange of knowledge assets.

knowledge flows: A firm's internal and external flows of knowledge.

knowledge management (KM): Knowledge management includes managing information (explicit/recorded knowledge); managing processes (embedded knowledge); managing people (tacit knowledge); managing innovation (knowledge conversion); and managing assets (intellectual capital) (David Skyrme, Nick Willard). Keeping data that have been aggregated orderly, and analyzing them for trends and other useful insights. Also known as "content management."

knowledge strategy: The organization's strategy for optimizing the internal and external knowledge as well as flows in order to grow intellectual capital.

leading indicator: Early warning proactive indicators. In a cause/effect relationship, leading indicators cause an effect on the lagging indicators. An indicator can be leading in its nature in one situation, but lagging in another.

learning organization: A learning organization is one that enables frequent knowledge interaction and capitalizes on new knowledge created in these interactions. A learning organization is more than an "organization that learns." Building a learning organization means changing the company's culture, structure, processes, leadership and forms of cooperation. The term is coined by Peter M. Senge.

market price: The price at which seller and buyer are ready and willing to commit.

market value added (MVA): The difference between market value and invested capital. Sometimes measured as market capitalization less adjusted shareholders' equity. Also corresponds to static intellectual capital, excluding expectation value.

objectivity: An analytic approach that is supposedly characterized by statements lacking bias.

pacesetter: A person, group or thing that leads the way or serves as a model.

participant observation: A technique or process designed to collect information within a non-laboratory context that is at least partially determined by the observer's presence. Participant observation is therefore a methodology for design research. Its great advantage is that it allows for observation of groups with the self as a member of the group.

performance management: The use of information to help set agreed-upon performance goals and objectives, allocate resources, prioritize projects and activities, align functional projects/activities with strategic goals and business objectives.

performance measurement: The ongoing process of assessing progress toward achieving predetermined goals and objectives.

premium value: The highest value that can be achieved. This value is reached when a client recognizes great talent, an unusually valuable process, or the potential for synergy in a relationship.

process: A carefully considered, precisely controlled and constantly improved sequence of steps or operations leading to a predetermined result (Office Productivity). Example: Hypertrack Process.

process capital: The combined value of both value creating and non-value creating processes. Gives reason for reorganization of design teams.

process management: A philosophy and a way to lead and organize a firm. The firm's operations are looked upon as a set of processes whose purpose is to produce goods or services that satisfy customers.

process-driven organization: An organization structured so that processes will work effectively. This kind of organization has processes as its backbone and is not built up around activities or functions (Office Productivity).

profitability: Most firms tend to minimize profits for tax purposes. Therefore, profits before distributions and taxes are the most meaningful figures, and profits have to be adjusted for any unusual or nonrecurring events.

real time management: Management for real time business. Characterized by minimizing response time to new circumstances and customer expectations.

re-engineering: A radical redesign of business processes to achieve improved results. Leads to best practice or failure. Re-engineering requires leadership wisdom.

relationship value: Human capital assessed according to the value it might create in combination with structural capital (also social capital).

staff utilization ratio: The ratio of billable hours divided by the total hours for all staff, expressed as a percentage.

strategic objective: Strategic goals that are in line with the mission. Strategic objectives are high level goals that are divided into different focus areas in the balanced scorecard grid.

synergism: The simultaneous action of separate firms that, together, have greater total effect than the sum of their individual effects.

supply-chain management: Tracking the movement of and demand for components used to manufacture a product across a variety of potential and actual suppliers, otherwise known as the supply chain.

tacit knowledge: Tacit knowledge is highly personal and hard to formalize and communicate. Tacit knowledge consists of know-how and mental models, beliefs and perspectives (Ikujiro Nonaka).

team: A group of people working together with a shared vision.

team building: Visualizing benefits from working in a team context and thereby stimulating teamwork.

three-generation team (3 G-teams): Team consisting of cross-border members from different generations, professional backgrounds, functions and cultures.

time to market (TTM): The time it takes from when a firm has defined a client need to when it can begin meeting it with a new service or a new generation of an existing services.

valuation: The process of assessing firm value, theoretically defined as the present value of all future cash flows discounted at the appropriate cost of capital.

value: A measure of appreciation of some phenomenon. The value of goods and services can either be measured by the amount of money or other goods or services for which they can be exchanged. Value is what someone wants and is willing to pay to get it.

value added: Operating result after depreciation, plus wage costs, payroll overheads and business development costs.

value chain: A generic model to analyze activities and costs in a company as well as in entities further up and down the chain. The model originates from work by Michael E. Porter.

value creation: Refinement and transformation of human capital, customer capital and organizational capital through mutual collaboration, into financial as well as non-financial value. A direct result of how people generate and apply knowledge.

value driver: An aspect of the organization that has been identified as providing significant future value; it indicates the firm's competitive advantage.

value networks: A social fabric for the fair exchange of tangibles and intangibles (Verna Allee).

values: Conceptions, explicit or implicit, distinctive of an individual or characteristic of a group, of the desirable which influences the selection from available modes, means and ends of actions.

ABOUT THE AUTHORS

James P. Cramer, Hon. AIA, Hon. IIDA, CAE, is the Chairman/CEO of The Greenway Group, a management consulting and research firm based in Atlanta. He is the author of *Design plus Enterprise, Seeking a New Reality in Architecture and Design*, editor of the monthly newsletter *Design Intelligence*, and co-editor of the annual *Almanac of Architecture & Design*. He is adjunct professor of architecture at the University of Hawaii, Manoa and co-chair of the Design Futures Council. The former executive vice president/CEO of The American Institute of Architects in Washington D.C., he has degrees from Northern State University, the University of St. Thomas, and postgraduate studies at the Wharton School of Business. He lives in Dunwoody, Georgia, with his wife Corinne Aaker Cramer.

Scott Simpson, FAIA, is president and CEO of The Stubbins Associates, Inc. in Cambridge, Massachusetts. A senior fellow and co-chair of the Design Futures Council, a think-tank based in Washington, D.C., he is a frequent speaker at seminars and conferences and has published more than 70 articles dealing with issues of innovation in the design professions. He is also an editor-at-large of *DesignIntelligence*. He has been a design critic at Yale University and the University of Wisconsin and a guest lecturer at the Harvard Graduate School of Design. His academic background includes degrees from both Harvard and Yale. He lives in a house of his own design in Carlisle, Massachusetts, with his wife Nancy Kuziemski.

Richard Swett, FAIA, architect, former ambassador, and former congressman, he is a fellow of The American Institute of Architects and a senior fellow of the Design Futures Council. He serves on numerous boards and is the state chair of the U.S. Olympic Committee. The former U.S. ambassador to Denmark, he is a senior counselor at APCO Worldwide, a global strategic communication and public relations firm, and is a senior advisor at Greenway Consulting. He received his Bachelor's degree in architecture from Yale University. He was bestowed the Grand-Croix of the Order of the Dannebrog, the Danish equivalent of knighthood, from Queen Margrethe II of Denmark. He lives in Bow, New Hampshire, with his wife Katrina Lantos Swett.

AVAILABLE FROM GREENWAY...

How Firms Succeed: A Field Guide to Design Management,
James P. Cramer and Scott Simpson.

A hands-on guide to running any design-related business—from a two-person graphics team to middle-management to CEOs of multinational firms—offering advice on specific problems and situations and providing insight into the art of inspirational management and strategic thinking.

"*How Firms Succeed* is a fountainhead of great ideas for firms looking to not just survive, but thrive in today's challenging marketplace.
—Thompson E. Penney, FAIA
President/CEO, LS3P Architecture, Interior Architecture, Land Planning and President, The American Institute of Architects, 2003

Design plus Enterprise: Seeking a New Reality in Architecture & Design, James P. Cramer.

Using specific examples, *Design plus Enterprise* illustrates how using business principles architects can create better design services—and thereby, a better society. It also demonstrates how smart design can drive economic success.

"This is must reading for every architect...It clearly points out how design and the designer are enriched by recognizing that the profession of architecture is both a business and a way of enhancing the environment"
—M. Arthur Gensler, Jr., FAIA
Chairman, Gensler Architecture, Design & Planning Worldwide

Almanac of Architecture & Design, James P. Cramer and Jennifer Evans Yankopolus, editors.

The only complete annual reference for rankings, records, and facts about architecture, interior design, landscape architecture, industrial design, and historic preservation.

"The reader who uses this book well will come away with a richer sense of the texture of the profession and of the architecture it produces."
—Paul Goldberger, *The New Yorker*

DesignIntelligence

The Design Futures Council's monthly "Report on the Future" provides access to key trends and issues on the cutting edge of the design professions. Each month it offers indispensable insight into management practices that will make any firm a better managed and more financially successful business.

"We read every issue with new enthusiasm because the information always proves so timely. No other publication in our industry provides as much useful strategy information."
—Davis Brody Bond LLP

—Order form on back—

ORDER FORM

How Firms Succeed: A Field Guide to Design Management: $39

Design plus Enterprise: $29

Almanac of Architecture & Design: $49.50

DesignIntelligence (including a one-year membership to the Design Futures Council): $289 annually

Shipping: $4.95
(add $1.50 per additional title)

NOTE: Shipping is included with DesignIntelligence—there is NO additional charge

Title	Quantity	Price:
	Shipping	

❑ Check ❑ Credit card Order Total

Card #   Expiration   Signature

Contact/Shipping Information

Name   Company

Address

City   State   Zip

Telephone   Fax

Email

Please fax this form to Greenway Communications: (770) 209-3778
or mail: Greenway Communications, 30 Technology Parkway South, Suite 200,
Norcross, GA 30092. For additional information call (800) 726-8603.

östberg ™

Library of Design Management

Every relationship of value requires constant care and commitment. At Östberg, we are relentless in our desire to create and bring forward only the best ideas in design, architecture, interiors, and design management. Using diverse mediums of communications, including books and the Internet, we are constantly searching for thoughtful ideas that are erudite, witty, and of lasting importance to the quality of life. Inspired by the architecture of Ragnar Östberg and the best of Scandinavian design and civility, the Östberg Library of Design Management seeks to restore the passion for creativity that makes better products, spaces, and communities. The essence of Östberg can be summed up in our quality charter to you: "Communicating concepts of leadership and design excellence."